Copyright © 2024 Andrea Oliver

All rights reserved

The characters and events portrayed in this book are fictitious. Any similarity to real persons, living or dead, is coincidental and not intended by the author.

No part of this book may be reproduced, or stored in a retrieval system, or transmitted in any form or by any means, electronic, mechanical, photocopying, recording, or otherwise, without express written permission of the publisher.

Cover design by: Art Painter
Library of Congress Control Number: 2018675309
Printed in the United States of America

I0513100

CONTENTS

Copyright	
Introduction: The Power of Purpose in Business	1
Chapter 1	3
Chapter 2	9
Chapter 3	17
Chapter 4	26
Chapter 5	34
Chapter 6	42
Chapter 7	51
Chapter 8	60
Chapter 9	69
Chapter 10	79
Chapter 11	87
Chapter 12	96
Chapter 13	104
Chapter 14	112
A Call to Action for Entrepreneurs and Investors	123

INTRODUCTION: THE POWER OF PURPOSE IN BUSINESS

In today's world, business is no longer just about profit. It's about building something meaningful, something that contributes to a larger purpose and creates real, lasting change. Entrepreneurs and investors alike are realizing that success doesn't have to come at the expense of people or the planet. In fact, the most resilient, impactful businesses are often those that prioritize social good alongside financial returns.

This book is for those who want to do more than build a business—they want to be part of a movement, a transformative shift in how we think about success. It's for the entrepreneurs ready to launch purpose-driven ventures and the investors eager to fund companies that align with their values. Together, you have the power to redefine what it means to thrive in today's complex world.

In these pages, we'll break down what it means to create a business with impact. You'll find that social entrepreneurship isn't about giving up profit for purpose or choosing one over the other. It's about building something sustainable, something that meets real needs in the market and in society. We'll explore the essential steps to launching and scaling a purpose-driven venture, from crafting your mission to measuring your impact and engaging like-minded partners.

Whether you're starting from scratch or looking to invest in businesses that make a difference, this book will guide you through the process. You'll discover strategies, tools, and stories from entrepreneurs and investors who have already set out on this path, navigating both the triumphs and challenges that come with building a better world through business.

So, if you're ready to create change and build something that matters, let's dive in. Together, let's explore how to turn purpose into action and action into lasting impact.

Part 1

Understanding the Power of Impact-Driven Business

CHAPTER 1

Why Social Entrepreneurship is the Future

The Rise of Purpose-Driven Ventures

Over the past few decades, the concept of social entrepreneurship has evolved from a niche idea into a powerful force for change. It's become clear that business can be more than just a profit-making machine—it can actually drive solutions to some of the world's biggest problems, from climate change to poverty to inequality. And if there's one thing that the 21st century has shown us, it's that people are hungry for change.

Let's start with a quick snapshot of what we mean by "social entrepreneurship." Social entrepreneurship isn't just about running a business that occasionally donates to charity or "goes green" by reducing its energy usage. No, social entrepreneurship is about businesses that embed a social or environmental mission at their core. These are companies that exist to solve problems. And more often than not, the drive to make a difference is what makes these businesses stand out.

A Story of Social Impact: The Origins of TOMS

One of the most famous examples of social entrepreneurship comes from a company you've likely heard of: TOMS Shoes. In the early 2000s, Blake Mycoskie, the founder of TOMS, was traveling in Argentina and noticed something troubling: a lot of children in impoverished areas didn't have shoes. Walking around barefoot, these kids faced all sorts of health risks and had limited access to schools that required shoes as part of the dress code.

This sparked an idea. Mycoskie realized he could launch a business that provided shoes to these children, but he didn't want to rely on donations. Instead, he built a for-profit company with a social mission: for every pair of shoes sold, TOMS would donate a pair to a child in need. It was the birth of the buy-one-give-one model, and it quickly resonated with consumers who loved the idea that their purchase could directly help someone else.

TOMS wasn't just selling shoes. They were selling purpose. And they weren't the only ones. Around the same time, we saw other companies emerging with similar models, like Warby Parker's vision program (which donates a pair of glasses for every pair purchased) and Bombas socks, which donates a pair of socks to homeless shelters for each pair sold. These companies proved that purpose-driven businesses weren't just good for society—they were also profitable.

Why Purpose is a Game-Changer

Today, businesses with purpose are popping up all over the world, and for good reason. Purpose-driven companies are built to solve real issues, and because of that, they often attract passionate, loyal customers who want to be part of something meaningful. The TOMS and Warby Parker models are great examples of how consumers can be partners in a company's mission, not just buyers of its products.

Think about it: when you buy a pair of TOMS shoes, you're not just adding a new item to your wardrobe. You're helping a child get their first pair of shoes. When you buy from Warby Parker, you're helping someone in a developing country see clearly for the first time. This shared purpose creates a bond between the brand and the customer that goes beyond the product itself. It's powerful, and it's why people are so drawn to purpose-driven companies.

But it's not just consumers who love purpose-driven businesses.

Investors are starting to see their value, too. As it turns out, businesses built on purpose are often more resilient in tough times. Take Patagonia, for example. This outdoor apparel brand has a laser-focused mission on environmental sustainability. They encourage customers to buy only what they need, offer repairs to extend the life of products, and even advocate for environmental policies that might seem at odds with traditional profit-making. And yet, they're incredibly successful, with loyal customers who respect their mission and make a point to support it.

The Dual Value of Profit and Purpose

Here's where social entrepreneurship really shines: combining profit and purpose. Traditionally, we thought of business and charity as two separate worlds. Business made money, and charity made a difference. But social entrepreneurship brings these two worlds together, proving that you don't have to choose between making a living and making an impact.

Case Study: Patagonia's Pledge to the Planet

Let's dive deeper into Patagonia's story. Founded by Yvon Chouinard in 1973, Patagonia has always focused on sustainability. But in 2022, Chouinard took things even further by transferring ownership of the entire company to a trust. Now, instead of benefiting a single family, Patagonia's profits go directly toward fighting climate change and protecting the planet. This bold move made headlines worldwide, with people applauding Patagonia's commitment to its mission.

Here's the kicker: Patagonia is still wildly profitable. In fact, the company's revenue has only grown as its environmental mission has become more central to its brand. People want to buy from companies they believe in. They want to feel like their money is supporting something bigger. This is the dual value of profit and purpose at work. It's not about sacrificing one for the other—it's about aligning them.

How Purpose Fuels Financial Success

Businesses built on purpose often have a significant advantage when it comes to resilience. During economic downturns, consumers still support companies they feel connected to because those companies stand for something they care about. Research has shown that companies with strong social missions are better at attracting and retaining employees, too. People want to work for companies that make a difference, not just a profit. This means that social enterprises tend to have highly motivated teams who are genuinely passionate about the company's success.

Take Bombas socks, for example. The founders discovered that socks were the most requested item in homeless shelters, so they built a company around addressing that need. For every pair of socks sold, Bombas donates a pair to someone in need. Since its founding, Bombas has donated tens of millions of socks, and the company has grown into one of the most popular sock brands in the U.S. Their model has proven that a commitment to purpose doesn't just bring in customers—it inspires everyone involved, from employees to investors.

For investors, purpose-driven businesses offer a different kind of value. Sure, they can bring in returns, but they also contribute to positive change. Impact investing—a form of investing focused on companies that aim for social and environmental benefits alongside financial gain—is on the rise. Investors see that putting money into companies like Bombas or Patagonia isn't just good for the wallet; it's good for the world.

Entrepreneurs and Investors as Change-Makers

This is where you come in. Whether you're an entrepreneur looking to start a purpose-driven business or an investor interested in making an impact, you have the power to change the world. Social entrepreneurship is about creating solutions where there are none, bringing hope to communities that need it, and addressing challenges that have been ignored for too long.

A Tip for Entrepreneurs: Start with Why

If you're an entrepreneur, the first step is to figure out your "why." Why do you want to start this business? What problem are you trying to solve? Social entrepreneurship isn't easy—it requires resilience, patience, and often a willingness to take risks. But when you have a clear "why," it gives you the strength to push through the tough times. Take time to think about the causes you care about most, whether it's environmental conservation, health access, or educational equality.

A lot of the most successful social enterprises started because their founders saw a problem and couldn't stand by and do nothing. They wanted to be part of the solution. So, start with why. Define the impact you want to make. Then, think about how your business can help achieve that goal.

A Tip for Investors: Look Beyond the Bottom Line

As an investor, social entrepreneurship gives you a unique opportunity to back companies that are doing good. But investing in social enterprises requires a different mindset. It's not just about profits—it's about impact. When evaluating a social enterprise, look at their mission, their team's commitment to that mission, and the impact they're aiming for. Sure, you want a good return on your investment, but remember that the best social enterprises offer something more: they're creating real change.

Impact investors often talk about the "double bottom line," which measures both financial returns and social impact. If you're new to impact investing, look for funds or organizations dedicated to finding and supporting high-impact businesses. The Global Impact Investing Network (GIIN) and B Lab (the nonprofit behind B

Corp certification) are great places to start learning about the impact investment world.

The Future is Bright for Purpose-Driven Ventures

The future of business is about more than just transactions—it's about relationships, responsibility, and resilience. Purpose-driven companies are built to last because they have something that traditional businesses often lack: a mission that matters. They're more than just brands; they're movements.

We're at a point in history where people are demanding more from companies. They want transparency, responsibility, and a commitment to making the world better. This is a huge opportunity for entrepreneurs and investors alike. By supporting and building businesses with impact, we're not only creating financial value but also laying the groundwork for a more sustainable, equitable world.

If you're ready to take that step, this book is your guide. We'll walk you through the process of defining your mission, building a sustainable business model, measuring your impact, and finding the resources and funding you need to make it all happen. Whether you're here to launch a new venture or invest in one, you're in the right place.

So let's get started. The world needs more entrepreneurs and investors who believe that business can be a force for good. Are you ready to be one of them?

CHAPTER 2

What Sets Social Entrepreneurship Apart

If you're here, you probably already sense that social entrepreneurship is something different. It's not just about building a business, and it's not quite the same as running a nonprofit. Social entrepreneurship sits at this unique intersection of profit and purpose, where a business can make money while solving social and environmental problems. And honestly, it's a beautiful place to be.

Social entrepreneurship challenges a lot of what we think we know about business and impact. It says you can have your cake and eat it, too. You can make a profit *and* make a difference. In this chapter, we'll dive deep into what makes social entrepreneurship distinct, the principles that drive it, and why it's so much more than just a "feel-good" business model. By the end, you'll understand exactly what sets social entrepreneurship apart and, hopefully, feel even more inspired to join this growing movement.

Defining Social Entrepreneurship and Its Scope

First off, let's clarify what we mean by social entrepreneurship. In simple terms, social entrepreneurship is about using business principles to create positive change. It's the fusion of a for-profit model with a nonprofit mindset, and it aims to solve social or environmental issues in ways that are sustainable and scalable. But to understand social entrepreneurship, it's helpful to compare it to traditional business models and nonprofits.

The Traditional Business Model vs. Social Enterprises

Traditional businesses are primarily driven by profit. There's nothing inherently wrong with that—after all, making money is a powerful motivator. But in a traditional business model, social or environmental impact is usually secondary, if it's even a consideration at all. Traditional businesses focus on maximizing shareholder value, often at the expense of the planet or people.

Social enterprises flip this idea on its head. Instead of asking, "How much money can we make?" they ask, "How much positive impact can we create?" The difference in motivation leads to a different kind of business altogether. A social enterprise might sell products or services, just like a traditional business, but every sale is designed to further a social or environmental cause. And yes, they still want to make a profit, but the profit is a means to an end—not the end itself.

How Social Enterprises Differ from Nonprofits

Nonprofits, on the other hand, operate with a mission as their primary driver, much like social enterprises. They raise funds through donations, grants, and sponsorships, which they then use to carry out their mission. The main difference? Nonprofits rely on external funding, while social enterprises generate their own income.

Social enterprises don't just give away products or services for free, like nonprofits sometimes do. Instead, they sell them, using the revenue to sustain and scale their operations. This is a game-changer because it makes social enterprises more sustainable in the long run. Instead of constantly seeking donations or funding, they're able to support themselves—and that's powerful.

Case Study: Warby Parker and Their "Buy a Pair, Give a Pair" Model

Warby Parker is a classic example of how social enterprises operate differently. This eyeglass company's mission isn't just to make stylish, affordable eyewear. Their deeper purpose is to help provide vision to those who don't have access to it. For every pair of glasses sold, Warby Parker donates a pair to someone in need.

Think about the brilliance of this model: Warby Parker doesn't have to rely on grants or donations to fund their vision programs. Every sale helps pay for the next pair of donated glasses. This self-sustaining model is the essence of social entrepreneurship, combining profitability with purpose. Warby Parker's business grows as its impact grows, proving that a successful business doesn't have to sacrifice social goals.

Core Principles and Goals of Social Entrepreneurship

Now that we've clarified what social entrepreneurship is, let's dig into what makes it tick. There are a few key characteristics that set social enterprises apart from traditional businesses and nonprofits: sustainability, scalability, and community engagement. Let's break each one down.

1. Sustainability

Sustainability is the backbone of social entrepreneurship. Unlike nonprofits that rely on donations, social enterprises design their models to be financially self-sufficient. They're not just solving a problem temporarily; they're building a system that can support itself over the long term. This is critical because the most pressing issues—like poverty, education, and environmental degradation—aren't going away overnight. They need lasting solutions, and social enterprises are built to provide exactly that.

A Real-Life Example: Grameen Bank and Microfinance

Muhammad Yunus, founder of Grameen Bank, understood the importance of sustainability when he created a microfinance model in Bangladesh. Yunus noticed that people in impoverished communities had no access to traditional banking, which prevented them from starting businesses or improving their quality of life. So, he founded Grameen Bank to provide small loans (microloans) to those who were left out of the financial system.

But here's the genius part: Grameen Bank charged a low interest rate on these loans, creating a cycle where borrowers could repay their loans and the bank could lend that money to the next person. This self-sustaining model meant that Grameen didn't need constant donations to keep operating. Instead, the bank's impact grew with every loan that was repaid. Today, Grameen Bank has helped millions escape poverty, proving that sustainability is essential for real, lasting change.

2. Scalability

Scalability is all about impact that grows with the business. A scalable social enterprise isn't satisfied with solving a problem on a small scale; it designs its operations to expand and reach as many people as possible. The best social enterprises build in mechanisms that allow them to scale without losing sight of their mission.

Case Study: Solar Sister's Approach to Empowering Women in Africa

Solar Sister is a social enterprise that provides women in sub-Saharan Africa with solar-powered products, like lamps and phone chargers. These products help families who live off the electrical grid to access clean, affordable energy. But Solar Sister's model doesn't stop at providing products—they train women to sell them, empowering these women to become entrepreneurs in their own right.

This approach is inherently scalable. As more women join the Solar Sister network, the organization's impact spreads, bringing clean energy to more homes and creating economic opportunities for more women. Solar Sister doesn't just drop off solar lights and leave; they build an ecosystem that grows as more people join. This is scalability in action.

3. Community Engagement

Finally, social enterprises put community engagement at the heart of everything they do. Social entrepreneurs know that real change doesn't happen from the top down; it happens when people feel empowered to take ownership of solutions. So, social enterprises don't just ask, "What do you need?" They ask, "How can we work together to create solutions that work for you?"

Anecdote: Greyston Bakery and Open Hiring

Greyston Bakery, a New York-based social enterprise, exemplifies community engagement with its "open hiring" model. At Greyston, anyone who wants a job can get one—no interviews, no background checks. This approach removes barriers for people who may have a hard time finding work due to criminal records or other challenges.

Not only does this model provide jobs, but it also strengthens the local community by giving people a second chance. Greyston's impact goes beyond the bakery; they've created a ripple effect in the community by showing that a business can be inclusive and profitable at the same time. It's a beautiful example of how engaging with the community can drive both impact and success.

Shattering Myths About Social Entrepreneurship

Even with all of these amazing examples, social entrepreneurship is still surrounded by myths and misconceptions. Let's tackle a few of the big ones.

Myth #1: Social Enterprises Can't Be Profitable

One of the most pervasive myths about social entrepreneurship is that it's "charity" and not a real business. This couldn't be further from the truth. Social enterprises operate with the same goals as any other business: to generate revenue and achieve sustainability. The difference is that social enterprises use their revenue to fuel impact.

In fact, social enterprises often enjoy higher levels of customer loyalty because people love supporting businesses that align with their values. A 2020 survey by Zeno Group found that consumers are four to six times more likely to buy from, trust, and champion companies that they believe have a strong purpose. This loyalty translates to profitability.

Case Study: Ben & Jerry's—Profitable and Purpose-Driven

Ben & Jerry's ice cream has long been a socially responsible business, advocating for issues like environmental sustainability, fair trade, and social justice. And yet, they're also one of the most profitable ice cream brands in the world. How? Because their values resonate with consumers. When customers buy Ben & Jerry's, they feel like they're supporting a company that cares about the same things they do.

Ben & Jerry's proves that you can be profitable *and* make an impact. The key is building a brand that's true to its values, one that people trust and want to support.

Myth #2: Social Enterprises Only Operate as Nonprofits

Another myth is that social enterprises are just another type of nonprofit. In reality, social enterprises can take on a variety of structures. Some are traditional for-profit companies (like Ben & Jerry's) with a strong social mission, while others are certified B Corporations or L3Cs (low-profit limited liability companies) that exist somewhere between the nonprofit and for-profit worlds.

Tip: Choose the Right Structure for Your Mission

If you're considering starting a social enterprise, think carefully about what structure will best support your mission. A for-profit model might give you more flexibility and access to capital, but a nonprofit model might help you attract grants and donations. Each structure has its own advantages, so take the time to research and choose wisely.

Myth #3: Social Enterprises Can't Compete with Traditional Businesses

There's a lingering idea that social enterprises can't compete with "regular" businesses because they're somehow less competitive. But the reality is that social enterprises often *outperform* their traditional counterparts. Why? Because they have something that many businesses lack: a purpose that resonates with customers, employees, and investors alike.

Case Study: Who Gives a Crap

Who Gives a Crap is a social enterprise that sells eco-friendly toilet paper. It sounds simple, but their mission is profound: they donate half of their profits to building toilets and improving sanitation in communities without access to these essentials. The company has attracted a loyal following, not just because of their sustainable products, but because customers know their purchase is making a difference.

And guess what? Who Gives a Crap is thriving, competing directly with major brands in the $21 billion toilet paper industry. They're proof that social enterprises can not only hold their own but even excel in competitive markets when they have a compelling mission.

The Bottom Line: Why Social Entrepreneurship Stands

Out

Social entrepreneurship is all about challenging the status quo. It says, "We don't have to choose between making money and making a difference. We can do both." Social enterprises are designed to be self-sustaining, scalable, and deeply connected to the communities they serve. They're more than businesses—they're vehicles for change.

In a world where people are increasingly looking for purpose and authenticity, social entrepreneurship offers a new way forward. It's a model that proves business can be a force for good, that profit doesn't have to come at the expense of people or the planet. And perhaps most importantly, it shows that anyone with a good idea and a strong sense of purpose can create a positive impact.

As we continue our journey, remember this: social entrepreneurship is not just a business model. It's a movement. And if you're ready to be part of it, you're in for an incredibly rewarding journey. Let's keep going—there's a world to change.

CHAPTER 3

Impact Metrics and Return on Investment (ROI)

Let's face it: traditional businesses tend to evaluate success in simple terms—sales, profit margins, stock prices. It's easy to measure the money coming in and going out. But for social entrepreneurs, the stakes are different. Success isn't just about a healthy bottom line; it's about knowing your business is making a real difference. You want to know that the work you're doing is creating tangible, positive change. And here's the big question: *how do you measure impact?*

It's one thing to feel like you're making a difference. It's another to prove it. That's where impact metrics come in, and they're transforming the way we think about return on investment, or ROI, for purpose-driven businesses.

In this chapter, we'll dive into what it means to measure social impact alongside financial performance, why it's valuable to investors and businesses alike, and some real-world examples of companies that have managed to do this brilliantly. By the end, you'll understand not just how to measure impact, but why it's crucial for building a purpose-driven business that attracts loyal customers, inspired employees, and forward-thinking investors.

Beyond Financial Returns: Measuring Social Impact

When we talk about measuring impact, we're moving beyond the basics. Financial returns are only part of the equation; what really matters for a social enterprise is understanding the broader impact your business is having on the world. Are you reducing waste? Increasing access to education? Providing jobs to underserved communities? These are just a few examples of the "social returns" that many social enterprises focus on.

One of the most widely used metrics in social entrepreneurship is **Social Return on Investment (SROI)**, a tool that assigns a dollar value to the social or environmental benefits created by a business. SROI helps answer questions like, "How much good did this investment generate?" or "What's the social value of the outcomes we're achieving?"

Breaking Down SROI

SROI isn't just a feel-good metric. It's actually a structured, methodical way to measure impact. At its core, SROI calculates the financial equivalent of the social impact a company is creating. The formula may sound complicated, but the basic idea is straightforward: you take the value of the social benefits your business produces, divide it by the investment required to create that value, and voilà—you have your SROI.

Here's a simple example. Imagine a social enterprise that's working to provide job training for formerly incarcerated individuals. The costs of running this program might include things like staffing, materials, and facility rentals. But the benefits—fewer people returning to prison, higher employment rates, improved community health—are enormous. These benefits can be assigned a financial value, giving investors and stakeholders a concrete understanding of the business's impact.

SROI isn't the only metric out there, but it's one of the most popular because it gives an accessible, "dollars-and-cents" way to measure something that can feel intangible. And the best part? SROI can be applied to almost any kind of social enterprise, whether you're improving environmental outcomes, supporting education, or enhancing community health.

Tip: Don't let SROI or any other metric intimidate you. Measuring impact can be as simple as starting with a few basic data points and building from there. Think about what metrics will best show the change you're trying to create and go from there.

Other Ways to Measure Impact

Aside from SROI, there are several other ways to measure social impact, and each has its own strengths depending on your business model and goals:

- **Theory of Change (ToC):** This framework outlines the logical steps needed to achieve a desired impact. It's about mapping out your mission, inputs, activities, outputs, and, ultimately, your intended outcomes. ToC is especially useful for identifying the ripple effects of your work.
- **Impact Measurement and Management (IMM):** This is a systematic approach that focuses on tracking outcomes over time and using data to continuously improve. Think of it as a way to measure progress as your business grows.
- **Global Impact Investing Network (GIIN) IRIS+ Metrics:** The GIIN offers a library of standardized metrics (IRIS+) tailored for social and environmental impact. These metrics cover areas like clean energy, health, poverty reduction, and more, making it easier to communicate your impact to stakeholders.

Anecdote: A Small Nonprofit's Journey with Impact Measurement

A friend of mine started a small nonprofit aimed at providing after-school programs for kids in low-income neighborhoods. In the early days, they didn't have any formal metrics for impact. They knew they were doing something good, and parents and kids seemed happy. But when they tried to apply for grants, they kept getting turned down. "We need measurable outcomes," the grant officers would say.

So, they started small. They tracked things like attendance, grade improvements, and feedback from parents. Slowly, their impact started taking shape in numbers and stories they could share. Within a year, they were able to prove that 75% of the kids who participated in their programs had shown measurable improvement in school performance. With these metrics, they secured their first major grant.

The moral of the story? Even small efforts to measure impact can make a big difference. Start with what you can track, and build from there.

The Value in Social Impact: Why Investors are Paying Attention

Impact metrics aren't just useful for showing that you're making a difference—they're becoming essential for attracting investors. Here's why: more and more investors are recognizing that purpose-driven companies aren't just good for the world; they're also good for business. Today, socially responsible investment (SRI) and impact investing are booming, and a growing number of investors want to put their money into companies that align with their values.

Why Social Impact Matters to Investors

Investors have long looked at the "triple bottom line"—people, planet, and profit—as a framework for assessing a company's sustainability. But now, they're also looking for hard data on impact. This trend isn't just about ethics; it's about value. Studies have shown that purpose-driven companies tend to be more resilient, attract loyal customers, and benefit from positive brand reputation—all of which contribute to financial success.

Take, for example, the Global Impact Investing Network's (GIIN) 2020 survey, which found that nearly 90% of impact investors reported that their investments met or exceeded expectations. These investors aren't sacrificing returns for social good; they're finding that companies focused on impact can outperform the market.

Case Study: Unilever's Sustainable Living Brands

Unilever, one of the largest consumer goods companies in the world, has long championed social responsibility. They launched a "Sustainable Living" initiative, focusing on brands that are specifically designed to tackle social and environmental issues. These include brands like Dove (which promotes body positivity and self-esteem), Hellmann's (which focuses on reducing food waste), and Ben & Jerry's (known for its social activism).

What's fascinating is that Unilever's Sustainable Living brands aren't just feel-good projects—they're also the company's best-performing brands. In 2019, these brands grew 69% faster than the rest of Unilever's portfolio and accounted for 75% of the company's overall growth. Unilever's CEO noted that purpose-led brands are "future-proofing" the business, attracting both loyal customers and forward-thinking investors.

Tip for Entrepreneurs: If you're building a purpose-driven company, think about how your impact aligns with investor goals. Being able to clearly communicate your impact metrics can help you attract investors who see the long-term value in your mission.

The Long-Term Value of Impact-Driven Companies

One of the reasons impact-driven companies are so appealing to investors is that they offer something traditional businesses often lack: resilience. Purpose-driven companies attract loyal customers and passionate employees, which creates a foundation for long-term growth. And because they're focused on social good, they're often better prepared to weather economic and market challenges.

Anecdote: The Rise of Certified B Corporations

Certified B Corporations (B Corps) are for-profit companies that meet rigorous social and environmental standards. They've become a beacon for impact investors because the certification process requires companies to measure and report on their social and environmental performance. Think of B Corps as companies that are officially "mission-locked."

When Ben & Jerry's was acquired by Unilever, people worried that the ice cream brand's commitment to social justice would fall by the wayside. But as a B Corp, Ben & Jerry's has a legal commitment to consider the impact of their decisions on stakeholders, not just shareholders. This "mission lock" reassured both employees and customers that Ben & Jerry's would remain true to its values. For investors, this commitment to impact translates to a brand that inspires loyalty, advocacy, and sustainable growth.

Case Studies in Measurable Impact

Let's look at a few companies that have successfully used impact metrics to not only demonstrate their positive effect but also enhance their financial returns and brand position.

Case Study #1: Tesla's Carbon Emissions Impact

Tesla is best known for its electric vehicles (EVs), but its core mission goes much deeper: "to accelerate the world's transition to sustainable energy." One of Tesla's main impact metrics is the amount of carbon emissions its vehicles have helped avoid. By tracking and reporting these emissions reductions, Tesla can quantify its environmental impact—a powerful metric that resonates with environmentally conscious investors and customers.

In 2020, Tesla reported that its fleet had saved over 5 million metric tons of CO_2 emissions. This metric isn't just a nice statistic; it's a key component of Tesla's brand and investment appeal. Investors see these emissions savings as a testament to Tesla's long-term mission, and the market has responded by making Tesla one of the world's most valuable companies.

Case Study #2: Beyond Meat's Environmental Savings

Beyond Meat is a food tech company known for its plant-based meat substitutes. Their mission is to reduce the environmental impact of food production by offering meat alternatives. Beyond Meat has measured its impact by tracking the resources saved through their products compared to traditional meat. For example, they report that their burgers use 99% less water, 93% less land, and generate 90% fewer greenhouse gas emissions than beef burgers.

These impact metrics have been a game-changer. They appeal to environmentally conscious consumers and investors alike, and they've helped Beyond Meat stand out in a crowded market. In its IPO, Beyond Meat raised over $240 million and has continued to grow as one of the top players in the plant-based protein industry.

Case Study #3: Allbirds' Carbon Footprint Transparency

Allbirds, a footwear company known for its eco-friendly shoes, has made carbon footprint transparency a key part of its brand. Allbirds not only measures the carbon emissions of each product but also displays it to customers, much like a nutritional label. This transparency builds trust with customers and has helped Allbirds attract a loyal following.

For investors, Allbirds' commitment to reducing its carbon footprint makes it a promising long-term investment. The company's eco-friendly approach has become a strong selling point, allowing it to compete with major footwear brands despite its relatively small size.

Why Measuring Impact Isn't Just for Investors

While impact metrics are valuable for attracting investors, they're also crucial for guiding and improving your business. Think of it this way: if you're trying to make the world better, impact metrics are your road map. They help you see what's working, what isn't, and how you can amplify your impact as you grow.

Impact metrics create accountability, transparency, and direction. They help you avoid "mission drift" by keeping you focused on your goals. And, perhaps most importantly, they show customers, employees, and investors that you're serious about making a difference.

The Bottom Line: Impact Metrics as a Foundation for Growth

Impact metrics aren't just a nice-to-have; they're a must-have for any serious social entrepreneur. They're the proof of the good you're doing in the world, and they're the key to building a purpose-driven business that attracts loyal customers and inspired investors. With the right impact metrics, you're not just building a business—you're building a movement, a community of people who believe in what you're doing and want to see it succeed.

So, don't be afraid to dive into impact measurement. It may seem daunting, but start small, track what matters most, and let your metrics evolve with your business. In the end, your impact isn't just a number; it's the legacy you're leaving behind, one that proves the power of purpose-driven business to make a real, lasting difference.

Part 2
Designing and Launching an Impact-Driven Business

CHAPTER 4

Identifying Opportunities and Defining Purpose

Creating a business is like embarking on a grand adventure, and in the world of social entrepreneurship, the destination is something even bigger than financial success. The goal is to make a lasting difference, to create something that positively impacts lives and addresses real problems. But before setting out on this journey, there's a crucial first step: finding your purpose.

Purpose isn't just a buzzword; it's the heart and soul of every great social enterprise. But here's the catch: your purpose has to resonate with others, too. It has to align with what the world needs, with what people will support and invest in. This chapter is all about helping you discover that purpose, figure out where it intersects with market potential, validate your idea through research, and turn it all into a powerful mission statement. Let's dive in!

Finding Purpose in the Marketplace

When we talk about "finding purpose," it's tempting to think only in personal terms. After all, purpose often comes from our own experiences, values, and the issues we're passionate about. But for a social enterprise to thrive, purpose has to connect with a broader need, a problem others face, and one that people are motivated to solve.

Tip: Start with the Causes You Care About

Before we get into market research and data, let's get a little personal. Think about the issues that have impacted you or the people you care about. Maybe you've faced a specific challenge in your own life, or perhaps there's a cause you feel drawn to, even if you can't fully explain why. Start with these personal sparks—they're often the seeds of a purpose-driven business.

Anecdote: How Bombas Found Purpose in Socks

Bombas, a sock company with a social mission, is a great example of a purpose-driven business that started from a personal moment of realization. Founders Randy Goldberg and David Heath learned that socks were the most requested clothing item in homeless shelters, yet they were rarely donated. It hit them deeply, and they saw a simple way to make a difference: for every pair of socks sold, they would donate a pair to someone in need. This mission gave Bombas a purpose and a loyal customer base that shares their values.

Bombas didn't reinvent the wheel. They found a common, everyday product (socks) and built a mission around it. Their purpose connected with a problem many people might not have considered, and they gave customers a way to be part of the solution with every purchase.

Identifying Needs in the Marketplace

Once you have a cause in mind, it's time to look at the bigger picture. Ask yourself questions like: Are other people invested in this cause? Is there room in the market for a solution? Do people recognize this as a problem, and are they willing to support efforts to address it? In other words, think about where your passion meets an opportunity.

Case Study: Who Gives A Crap's Twist on Toilet Paper

Who Gives A Crap is another company that found purpose in an unexpected place: toilet paper. The founders, Simon Griffiths, Danny Alexander, and Jehan Ratnatunga, realized that sanitation was a huge issue worldwide. Approximately 2 billion people don't have access to toilets, leading to health and environmental problems.

But how could a business help? The founders launched a company selling eco-friendly toilet paper, with half of the profits going toward building toilets in underserved communities. They tapped into a universal need—everyone uses toilet paper—while connecting it to an urgent global issue. They found a way to turn a routine purchase into something that could change lives.

When finding your purpose in the marketplace, remember that it doesn't have to be revolutionary. Often, the best ideas are simple, everyday products or services combined with a purpose that resonates.

Conducting Impact-Driven Market Research

Once you've identified a cause you're passionate about, it's time to do your homework. This isn't just any kind of market research; it's *impact-driven* research. It's about validating your idea by exploring both the demand for your product or service and the potential for positive impact. Let's talk about how to approach this in a way that goes beyond just numbers and really dives into community needs.

Understand the Community You Want to Serve

The first step in impact-driven research is understanding the people you aim to help. Social entrepreneurship is about creating solutions that matter to communities, and this means listening to their voices. Are you solving a problem they care about? Will your solution actually meet their needs?

Tip: Go Directly to the Source

There's no better way to understand a community's needs than by talking to the people themselves. Conduct interviews, send out surveys, or even host focus groups. The insights you'll gain are invaluable—they can help you refine your product, shape your messaging, and, most importantly, ensure you're building something that resonates with real people.

Example: The Honest Company's Early Research

When Jessica Alba co-founded The Honest Company, her goal was to create non-toxic, environmentally friendly household products for families. But instead of just assuming that other people cared about these issues as much as she did, Alba and her team dug deep into market research. They found that parents were, indeed, worried about toxins in everyday products and that there was a huge demand for cleaner alternatives. By validating this need, The Honest Company built a business that's both impactful and in high demand.

The lesson? Don't just assume there's a need for your solution. Get out there and confirm it by engaging with the community you want to serve. Real-world insights will help you avoid blind spots and create something genuinely valuable.

Gauge Market Potential

Social impact is key, but it's not the only factor. Your idea also needs to be marketable. This means assessing things like the demand for your product, potential competition, and the willingness of customers to pay for your solution. To do this, look for patterns, study competitors, and, if possible, test the market with a small pilot.

Anecdote: Testing the Market with TOMS Shoes

Before officially launching TOMS, founder Blake Mycoskie wanted to see if people would actually buy into the "One for One" model. So, he started small. He made a few dozen pairs of shoes and tested them out in local shops and events. The response was overwhelmingly positive, giving him the confidence to move forward. This initial success helped TOMS gain momentum and refine its model before fully committing to production.

Testing the market, even on a small scale, is a great way to see if your idea has traction. It's also a chance to get feedback, learn, and adjust before investing heavily.

Analyze Competitors' Impact Models

You're not alone in the world of social entrepreneurship, and that's a good thing! Studying competitors' impact models can give you valuable insights into what works, what doesn't, and where there might be gaps in the market. Look at companies with similar missions or audiences and analyze their approach. Are they focusing on sustainability? Are they solving issues similar to yours? Can you identify an aspect of the problem that they're overlooking?

Example: Warby Parker and Eye Care Access

Warby Parker entered a market that already had plenty of big players in eyewear, but they differentiated themselves by combining affordable glasses with an impact model focused on vision care for underserved communities. They identified a gap in access to affordable eye care and built a business around filling that need. Their success is a reminder that even if the market is competitive, a unique impact-driven angle can help you stand out.

Building a Mission Statement with Impact

Once you've identified a cause and validated the need through research, it's time to translate all that passion and data into a mission statement. Your mission statement is the north star of your social enterprise. It guides everything you do, from product development to marketing to how you engage with customers. A good mission statement is short, clear, and packed with purpose.

The Basics of a Strong Mission Statement

A great mission statement does three key things:

1. **Clarifies your purpose:** It clearly states *why* your company exists.
2. **Defines your impact:** It shows *how* you plan to make a difference.
3. **Connects with your audience:** It resonates with the people you aim to serve or attract.

Example: Patagonia's Mission Statement

"Build the best product, cause no unnecessary harm, use business to inspire and implement solutions to the environmental crisis."

Patagonia's mission statement is a masterclass in simplicity and purpose. It tells you everything you need to know: they're focused on creating quality products, minimizing environmental harm, and using business as a tool for change. This mission statement doesn't just inspire customers; it serves as a constant reminder for Patagonia's team of what they're working toward.

Crafting Your Own Mission Statement

To write your mission statement, start by answering these questions:

- **What problem are we solving?** Describe the issue your business will address.
- **Who are we serving?** Identify the community or demographic you're working to impact.
- **What's our approach?** Explain how your business will tackle the problem in a unique or innovative way.

Once you've brainstormed your answers, try to summarize them in one to two sentences. Keep it clear and concise, but make sure it captures the heart of your purpose.

Anecdote: How Ten Thousand Villages Found Their Mission

Ten Thousand Villages, a fair-trade retailer, built its mission around supporting artisans in developing countries. Their goal was to help these artisans achieve sustainable incomes by connecting them with Western markets. After working with artisans, the founders developed a simple, powerful mission: "To create opportunities for artisans in developing countries to earn income by bringing their products and stories to our markets." This mission not only clarifies their purpose but also resonates with customers who want to support ethical shopping.

Testing Your Mission with Others

Once you have a draft of your mission statement, share it with a few trusted friends, colleagues, or potential customers. Ask them if it resonates, if it's clear, and if it captures what you're trying to achieve. Mission statements evolve, so don't worry if you need to tweak it a few times. The goal is to create something that feels authentic, inspiring, and true to your vision.

Tip: Keep Your Mission in Sight

A mission statement is only powerful if it's remembered. Keep your mission front and center in your business operations. Use it in your marketing materials, mention it in meetings, and revisit it regularly to make sure your business remains aligned with your purpose. A great mission isn't just words on a website—it's a guiding principle for everything you do.

Bringing It All Together

Identifying opportunities and defining your purpose is about balancing passion with practicality. It's finding that sweet spot where your desire to make a difference meets a real need in the market. Here's a quick recap:

1. **Start with What You Care About:** Identify causes that resonate with you and that you're genuinely excited to address.
2. **Conduct Impact-Driven Market Research:** Validate the need for your solution by understanding community needs, assessing market potential, and learning from competitors.
3. **Craft a Mission Statement That Inspires:** Write a mission that's clear, concise, and aligned with your goals. Make it your north star as you build and grow.

Creating a purpose-driven business isn't about being perfect from day one. It's about listening, learning, and aligning your work with values that go beyond profit. When you know your purpose, your decisions become clearer, your team becomes more motivated, and your customers become your biggest advocates.

This is just the beginning of building an impact-driven business. Armed with a clear purpose and mission, you're ready to start making meaningful strides toward positive change. Let's continue on this journey to make the world a better place, one purposeful step at a time.

CHAPTER 5

Crafting a Business Model for Purpose and Profit

Creating a purpose-driven business doesn't mean reinventing the wheel—but it does mean thinking differently about how you'll operate and grow. Building a social enterprise is about balancing two goals: making a meaningful impact and generating sustainable revenue. And here's the thing: you don't have to choose one over the other. In fact, the best social enterprises out there have found ways to do both, proving that purpose and profit can go hand in hand.

In this chapter, we're going to look at how to choose a business model that supports your mission, walk through how to use the Social Lean Canvas as a planning tool, and dive into strategies for ensuring that your impact and revenue grow in harmony over time. Ready to dig in?

Choosing a Business Model for Lasting Impact

When it comes to crafting a business model, social enterprises have an edge. You're not just selling a product or service; you're offering people a way to make a difference. But to succeed, you need a model that makes sense for your mission, your audience, and your long-term goals. Let's explore a few popular models that purpose-driven companies use to make an impact and generate revenue.

1. Subscription Services

Subscription models are all about building long-term relationships with your customers. For social enterprises, this model works particularly well because it creates a steady stream of revenue that can fund ongoing impact. By getting customers to subscribe, you're also engaging them in your mission over time, creating a sense of loyalty and shared purpose.

Case Study: Who Gives a Crap

Who Gives a Crap sells eco-friendly toilet paper, but it's so much more than that. The company was started with a mission to help improve sanitation and hygiene in underserved communities, with half of the profits going to build toilets in places that need them. By offering a subscription option, Who Gives a Crap makes it easy for customers to reorder toilet paper and continue supporting the mission without thinking twice.

The beauty of the subscription model here is that it makes giving effortless. Customers don't have to remember to make donations or take additional steps—they just sign up once, and every month, they're contributing to a good cause. The company gets reliable revenue, the mission gets ongoing funding, and the customers get a sense of being part of something bigger. It's a win-win.

2. Buy-One-Give-One

The buy-one-give-one (B1G1) model is almost synonymous with social entrepreneurship at this point, thanks to companies like TOMS and Warby Parker. The concept is simple but powerful: for every product sold, the company donates an equivalent item to someone in need. This model works well for products that fulfill basic needs, like shoes, glasses, and even food.

Case Study: TOMS Shoes and Warby Parker

TOMS is the classic example of this model. When founder Blake Mycoskie visited Argentina, he was struck by how many children didn't have shoes—a basic necessity that impacts health, school attendance, and self-esteem. He created TOMS with a one-for-one model, and the rest is history. Customers loved knowing that their purchase had a direct, tangible impact. And because the giving was built into the cost structure, TOMS could be both profitable and purposeful.

Warby Parker took a slightly different approach with their "Buy a Pair, Give a Pair" model. For every pair of glasses sold, Warby Parker provides a pair to someone who lacks access to eye care. Rather than just handing out glasses, they partner with local organizations to ensure that the distribution model is sustainable and culturally appropriate, which helps maximize the long-term impact.

Tip: The B1G1 model is incredibly appealing to consumers, but it's crucial to think about the logistics and costs. Consider if this model aligns with your product's pricing, your audience's expectations, and the communities you aim to help.

3. Shared-Value Approach

The shared-value approach is all about creating benefits for both the business and society. Instead of a straightforward buy-one-give-one or donation model, shared-value companies embed social good into their core operations. This model can take many forms—reducing environmental waste, supporting fair labor practices, or building products that address a specific social need.

Case Study: Patagonia's Environmental Mission

Patagonia's business model is based on shared value. They don't just sell outdoor clothing; they focus on making durable, sustainable products that minimize environmental impact. Patagonia has built a brand around responsible sourcing, fair labor, and environmental activism, going so far as to encourage customers to repair rather than replace their gear.

By integrating sustainability into their operations, Patagonia creates value not just for the company but also for the planet. This model resonates deeply with environmentally conscious customers who are willing to pay a premium for products that align with their values. The shared-value approach has allowed Patagonia to build a strong, loyal customer base while setting a high standard for environmental responsibility.

Utilizing the Social Lean Canvas

Once you have a sense of the model that might work best for your mission, it's time to get a bit more structured. The Social Lean Canvas is a fantastic tool for mapping out your business model with an emphasis on social impact. It's a variation of the popular Lean Canvas used by startups, but with added sections that consider social and environmental goals.

How the Social Lean Canvas Works

The Social Lean Canvas has nine sections, each one focusing on a critical component of your business:

1. **Problem** - Identify the social or environmental problem you're addressing.
2. **Customer Segments** - Define the people or groups who benefit from your solution.
3. **Unique Value Proposition** - Articulate what makes your solution special and impactful.
4. **Solution** - Describe how you're solving the problem.
5. **Channels** - Outline how you'll reach your customers and community.
6. **Revenue Streams** - List your sources of revenue.
7. **Cost Structure** - Identify the main costs associated with running your business.
8. **Impact Metrics** - Decide how you'll measure your im-

pact.
9. **Social/Environmental Benefit** - Highlight the long-term benefits your business will create.

By using the Social Lean Canvas, you can visualize both the impact and revenue sides of your business, ensuring that neither one overshadows the other. Let's go through an example to make this real.

Example: Applying the Social Lean Canvas to a Clean Water Initiative

Imagine you're starting a social enterprise that aims to provide affordable water filtration systems to communities with limited access to clean water. Here's how you might fill out the Social Lean Canvas:

- **Problem**: Millions of people lack access to clean drinking water, leading to health issues and poor quality of life.
- **Customer Segments**: Households in low-income regions, NGOs, schools, health clinics.
- **Unique Value Proposition**: Affordable, long-lasting water filtration systems that improve health and save lives.
- **Solution**: Develop a filtration system that uses local materials and is easy to maintain.
- **Channels**: Partnerships with NGOs, local distribution centers, and community outreach programs.
- **Revenue Streams**: Sales of filtration systems, partnerships with NGOs, grants.
- **Cost Structure**: Manufacturing, distribution, staff, training programs for local technicians.
- **Impact Metrics**: Number of units distributed, health improvements (e.g., reduced cases of waterborne diseases), community satisfaction.
- **Social/Environmental Benefit**: Healthier communities, reduced medical costs, and empowerment of local technicians.

The Social Lean Canvas helps you see the big picture without getting bogged down in too much detail. It's a quick and easy way to align your impact goals with your business goals, ensuring they're working in harmony.

Tip: The Social Lean Canvas is a living document. Revisit it regularly as your business grows to refine your strategy and adapt to new challenges.

Long-Term Sustainability and Growth

With your business model mapped out, the final piece of the puzzle is thinking about sustainability and growth. How do you ensure that your business not only survives but thrives over time? And more importantly, how do you grow without losing sight of your mission?

1. Build a Strong Financial Foundation

No matter how noble your mission is, financial stability is essential. Start by ensuring your revenue model is solid, and keep an eye on cash flow. Many social enterprises struggle because they put mission above everything, but it's a balancing act. Financial health allows you to keep making an impact—so don't be afraid to prioritize it.

Example: The Growth of The Honest Company

Jessica Alba's The Honest Company, which sells eco-friendly household products, started with a strong mission but also focused on financial growth. They understood that profitability would allow them to scale, reach more customers, and expand their impact. By building a financially sustainable model, The Honest Company has been able to grow without losing sight of its core mission of providing safe products for families.

2. Stay Mission-Driven as You Scale

Growth can bring a host of new challenges, and one of the biggest risks is "mission drift." As you bring in new investors, hire employees, or expand to new markets, there's a risk of losing focus on your original purpose. To avoid this, bake your mission into every aspect of your company's culture and operations.

Case Study: Ben & Jerry's Social Mission as They Expanded

When Ben & Jerry's was acquired by Unilever, there were concerns that the ice cream brand's social mission would be watered down. But Ben & Jerry's took steps to ensure that wouldn't happen. They set up an independent board to oversee social impact, and Unilever agreed to support their values. By protecting their mission during growth, Ben & Jerry's continued to be a force for good, championing issues like climate change, fair trade, and social justice.

3. Measure Impact and Adjust

Finally, growth isn't just about revenue. It's also about impact. Measuring your social impact is key to understanding whether you're staying true to your mission as you scale. Use metrics that matter to your community and stakeholders, and don't be afraid to adapt based on what you learn.

Anecdote: How a Local Food Rescue Organization Stayed True to Its Mission

A small food rescue organization started with a simple mission: reduce food waste and feed the hungry. As they grew, they realized that some of their original methods were too costly and didn't scale well. By measuring their impact (meals delivered, food waste reduced), they identified inefficiencies and made adjustments. Today, they're able to reach more people than ever while staying true to their purpose.

Bringing It All Together

Crafting a business model that balances purpose and profit is one of the most rewarding challenges you'll face as a social entrepreneur. By choosing a model that aligns with your mission, using tools like the Social Lean Canvas to guide your planning, and keeping an eye on long-term sustainability, you'll be building a foundation that can support both growth and impact.

Remember: a purpose-driven business isn't about choosing between making money and making a difference. It's about finding a way to do both. As you build and grow, stay connected to your mission, keep refining your model, and embrace the impact you're making. The world needs more businesses like yours—ones that are built not just to succeed, but to make a difference.

CHAPTER 6

Structuring the Business for Success

When you're building a business that's focused on making a difference, every decision has extra weight—especially the legal structure you choose. For social entrepreneurs, structuring a business goes beyond the typical "LLC vs. Corporation" debate. You're not just protecting your assets or planning for taxes; you're setting up a framework that reflects your mission and can help you attract investors, build credibility, and ultimately make a bigger impact.

In this chapter, we'll dig into the legal options for social enterprises, from B Corps to low-profit LLCs (L3Cs) and mission-driven corporations. We'll walk through the pros and cons of each structure, share tips on navigating the registration process, and explore certifications like B Corp that can enhance your business's credibility. Whether you're just starting or considering a legal restructuring, let's find the right fit for your impact-driven mission.

Legal Structures for Social Enterprises

When structuring a social enterprise, you're essentially balancing three goals: impact, profitability, and flexibility. Traditional business structures, like sole proprietorships and LLCs, work well for profit-driven ventures but can sometimes limit a social enterprise's ability to prioritize impact. Fortunately, there are now structures designed to support both mission and margin. Here's a rundown of the main options.

1. Benefit Corporation (B Corp)

Benefit Corporations, or B Corps, are for-profit companies that are legally committed to balancing profit and purpose. To become a B Corp, a business must amend its legal documents to include a commitment to creating a positive impact on society and the environment. B Corps have to meet high standards for transparency, accountability, and performance, and they're also required to report on their impact each year.

Case Study: Ben & Jerry's and Their B Corp Status

Ben & Jerry's is a famous example of a B Corp that balances profit with purpose. They didn't start as a B Corp (the structure didn't exist when they were founded), but once it became an option, they made the switch. This move aligned with their long-standing commitment to social justice, environmental responsibility, and fair trade sourcing. As a B Corp, Ben & Jerry's not only enjoys legal protection to pursue its mission, but it also signals to customers and investors that they're serious about impact.

The B Corp certification has created a global community of purpose-driven companies that share a commitment to "using business as a force for good." Today, there are over 4,000 certified B Corps around the world, and each has gone through rigorous assessments to show they're meeting the highest standards of social and environmental performance.

2. Low-Profit Limited Liability Company (L3C)

L3Cs are a hybrid structure that blends characteristics of non-profits and for-profits, making them a popular choice for social enterprises focused on public benefit. The goal of an L3C is to generate a modest profit while pursuing a mission-driven purpose. Unlike traditional LLCs, L3Cs have a legal obligation to prioritize mission over profit, which makes them particularly appealing to foundations and impact investors.

Example: The L3C Model in Action

A real-life example of an L3C is Earthwise Organics, a company that promotes sustainable agriculture and environmental education. Earthwise Organics operates as an L3C, which allows them to attract mission-aligned investors who are more interested in the social benefits than the financial returns. The L3C structure helps Earthwise stay focused on its mission of environmental education while still being a viable business.

The L3C structure is particularly advantageous for companies seeking "program-related investments" from foundations. In the U.S., foundations can make grants or investments in L3Cs that support charitable activities, helping social enterprises secure funding that wouldn't be available to a traditional LLC or corporation.

3. Mission-Driven Limited Liability Company (LLC)

Mission-driven LLCs are a more flexible option for social entrepreneurs who want to maintain control over the business while also committing to a purpose beyond profit. Unlike B Corps, mission-driven LLCs don't require formal certification or reporting, but the owner can still write a mission into the company's operating agreement to ensure it's a priority.

Anecdote: A Small Business With a Big Mission

A friend of mine launched a zero-waste grocery store as a mission-driven LLC. By structuring her business as an LLC, she maintained flexibility, which was crucial as she figured out the logistics of sourcing, packaging, and selling eco-friendly products. She wrote a commitment to sustainability into her operating agreement, so her mission was legally recognized even though she wasn't a certified B Corp. This allowed her to pursue her purpose without the formal requirements of a B Corp or L3C.

Mission-driven LLCs are ideal for smaller social enterprises or those just getting started. They allow you to focus on your mission without a lot of additional paperwork or regulations, making it a good option if you need flexibility to grow.

4. Nonprofit Organization with Earned Revenue

This isn't a legal structure on its own, but it's worth mentioning. Many social enterprises start as nonprofits but generate revenue by selling products or services. This approach allows nonprofits to support their mission with self-generated income rather than relying solely on donations and grants.

For example, a nonprofit focused on art education might sell art supplies or workshops to fund its programs. By building an earned revenue stream, the nonprofit reduces its dependency on external funding and gains financial stability, which helps it expand its impact.

Tip: If you're considering the nonprofit route, think about whether your enterprise could generate revenue from activities that align with your mission. Earned revenue can give nonprofits much-needed flexibility while supporting long-term sustainability.

Pros and Cons of Each Structure

Each structure has its advantages and drawbacks, and the best choice depends on factors like your mission, funding goals, and operational needs. Let's break down some key pros and cons for each option.

Benefit Corporation (B Corp)

- **Pros:**
    - Legal protection for mission-driven activities,

    even if they impact profit.
    - Credibility with customers, investors, and employees who prioritize social impact.
    - Access to the global B Corp community and resources.
- **Cons:**
    - Annual impact reporting can be time-consuming.
    - B Corp certification and assessments may require fees and administrative work.
    - May deter traditional investors focused solely on financial returns.

Low-Profit Limited Liability Company (L3C)

- **Pros:**
    - Attracts mission-aligned funding, especially from foundations.
    - Legally committed to prioritizing social mission over profit.
    - Flexible for social entrepreneurs who need investor funding without losing control of their mission.
- **Cons:**
    - Only recognized in certain U.S. states (availability may vary by location).
    - May have limited appeal to high-return investors, as it's structured to generate moderate profit.
    - Lacks the brand recognition and network of B Corps.

Mission-Driven LLC

- **Pros:**
    - Flexibility to adapt and grow without specific regulatory requirements.
    - Ability to incorporate a mission into the company's operating agreement without certification.
    - Easier to manage than B Corps or L3Cs, with

fewer regulatory demands.
- **Cons**:
  - No legal protection for mission-driven activities that could impact profitability.
  - May lack the credibility of a certified B Corp or nonprofit.
  - Limited ability to attract impact-focused investors or funding from foundations.

Nonprofit with Earned Revenue

- **Pros**:
  - Access to grants, donations, and tax-exempt status for certain activities.
  - Financial stability through earned revenue reduces reliance on donations.
  - Mission is the priority, which can appeal to impact-driven stakeholders.
- **Cons**:
  - Revenue-generating activities may be restricted by nonprofit regulations.
  - Can be challenging to secure traditional investment capital.
  - Complex tax implications, especially if there's a significant earned revenue component.

Steps to Registration and Certification

Once you've chosen a structure, it's time to make it official. The process varies by structure and location, but here's a general overview of what to expect, along with tips for navigating registration and certification.

1. Registering a Benefit Corporation (B Corp)

To register as a Benefit Corporation, you'll first need to incorporate your business as a corporation in your state. From there, you'll amend the articles of incorporation to include a commitment to creating public benefit. Here's a quick breakdown:

- **Step 1**: Incorporate as a traditional corporation in your state.
- **Step 2**: Amend your articles of incorporation to include your mission and commitment to public benefit.
- **Step 3**: Submit annual benefit reports (requirements vary by state).

For those looking for B Corp certification, you'll go a step further by taking the **B Impact Assessment**. This rigorous assessment covers everything from employee benefits and diversity to environmental impact and community engagement. Once you pass the assessment, you can officially become a Certified B Corp.

Tip: The B Impact Assessment is thorough and can take time, so start early. It's free to take, and even if you're not ready for certification, the assessment will give you insights into areas where your business can improve.

2. Registering an L3C

L3Cs are similar to LLCs in terms of structure and flexibility, but they include language in their operating agreement stating that mission takes priority over profit. Here's a basic registration process:

- **Step 1**: Confirm that your state allows L3Cs (currently available in a limited number of U.S. states).
- **Step 2**: Draft an operating agreement that includes your mission as the primary purpose.
- **Step 3**: File articles of organization with your state, designating your business as an L3C.

If your state doesn't recognize L3Cs, you can consider structuring as a mission-driven LLC and writing the mission into your operating agreement.

3. Setting Up a Mission-Driven LLC

Setting up a mission-driven LLC is one of the simplest options:

- **Step 1**: Register as an LLC in your state.
- **Step 2**: Draft an operating agreement that includes your mission as a core value or purpose.
- **Step 3**: Operate with flexibility while keeping your mission front and center.

For smaller social enterprises or those just starting out, this is an accessible way to integrate mission without a lot of regulatory demands.

4. Registering a Nonprofit with Earned Revenue

Nonprofits have a different registration process and additional compliance requirements. Here's a brief look at the process:

- **Step 1**: Incorporate as a nonprofit in your state, following your state's guidelines for charitable organizations.
- **Step 2**: Apply for 501(c)(3) tax-exempt status with the IRS (in the U.S.), which requires a detailed application and compliance with strict rules regarding profit.
- **Step 3**: Set up earned revenue streams within the constraints of nonprofit regulations.

Remember that nonprofits with earned revenue must carefully manage any profit to avoid conflicts with their tax-exempt status.

Bringing It All Together

Choosing the right structure for your social enterprise isn't a decision to take lightly. Each option has unique benefits and challenges, so think about your mission, your growth goals, and your funding needs. The right structure will not only protect your mission but also position your business for long-term success.

Remember, no structure is perfect. It's about finding the best fit for where you are now, and knowing that you can adapt as your enterprise grows. Your mission deserves a solid foundation, and choosing the right structure is the first step in building a business that can stand the test of time.

CHAPTER 7

Acquiring or Partnering with Aligned Businesses

Creating a successful social enterprise often means building more than just a product or service; it means building connections. One of the most powerful ways to expand your impact and bring your vision to life is through partnerships or acquisitions with businesses that share your mission. A strategic acquisition or a well-structured partnership can help you scale, access new markets, share resources, and ultimately amplify your impact.

In this chapter, we'll explore the advantages of acquisitions and partnerships, share tips for assessing compatibility, and provide strategies for structuring partnerships that maximize impact. Whether you're just starting out or looking to grow, learning how to leverage existing resources and align with others can be a game-changer.

Advantages of Acquisition and Strategic Partnerships

Think of partnerships and acquisitions as a shortcut to growth. Instead of building everything from scratch, you're joining forces with others who've already laid some groundwork. Strategic partnerships and acquisitions give you access to resources, expertise, and networks you might not have on your own, all while helping you scale your impact faster. Here are a few key advantages of each approach.

1. Leveraging Existing Infrastructure

Acquiring or partnering with an established company means you don't have to reinvent the wheel. Maybe they have a production facility, distribution channels, or a customer base that you can tap into. By acquiring or joining forces, you're getting a head start with access to resources and systems already in place.

Example: Ben & Jerry's Acquisition by Unilever

One of the most famous examples of a social enterprise acquisition is Ben & Jerry's. When Unilever acquired the company, it allowed Ben & Jerry's to expand its reach globally while keeping its commitment to social justice, environmental sustainability, and community impact. Unilever provided access to production facilities and distribution networks that Ben & Jerry's couldn't have accessed alone, enabling them to make a larger impact. The acquisition allowed Ben & Jerry's to grow without sacrificing its values, and Unilever benefited from aligning with a socially responsible brand beloved by customers.

2. Expanding Market Reach

Partnering with or acquiring another business can also be a way to reach a new market. Imagine you're a sustainable fashion brand in the U.S., and you want to enter the European market. Partnering with an eco-conscious retailer based in Europe can help you get established there more quickly, with less risk.

Case Study: Patagonia's Partnership with Yerdle

Patagonia, the outdoor apparel company known for its environmental activism, partnered with Yerdle, a company specializing in product resale. Together, they launched Patagonia Worn Wear, a program that encourages customers to trade in and buy used Patagonia products. This partnership allowed Patagonia to expand its sustainability efforts and reduce waste, aligning perfectly with its mission. Yerdle provided the technology and expertise in resale, while Patagonia brought its brand and loyal customer base, making it a win-win for both parties.

3. Sharing Resources and Reducing Costs

In the world of social impact, resources are often limited. Strategic partnerships can help alleviate this by sharing costs, whether it's marketing expenses, product development, or customer service. Pooling resources means both businesses can operate more efficiently, leaving more budget and energy to focus on making a difference.

Anecdote: Small Local Food Co-Ops Joining Forces

In my hometown, a group of small, local food co-ops decided to partner to share resources. Each co-op had its own customer base, but they were all passionate about supporting local farmers, promoting organic food, and reducing environmental impact. By partnering, they were able to share distribution trucks, marketing efforts, and even bulk purchases from suppliers, lowering costs across the board. This allowed each co-op to remain financially stable while growing their collective impact on the local community and environment.

Evaluating Mission Alignment

One of the trickiest parts of partnering with or acquiring another business is ensuring that your missions align. Mission alignment is crucial because if your values don't match, it can lead to conflicts, confusion, and ultimately, a loss of trust with your customers. Here are some practical steps to assess whether a potential partner or acquisition is truly compatible with your mission.

1. Define Your Non-Negotiables

Before even starting conversations with a potential partner or acquisition target, make sure you're clear about your own mission and values. What are your non-negotiables? What are you willing to compromise on? Knowing this upfront will help you assess whether the other business aligns with your values.

Tip: Write Down Your Core Values

Grab a piece of paper and write down the core values that drive your social enterprise. Whether it's sustainability, ethical labor practices, or community empowerment, list these values out and keep them visible during discussions with potential partners. This will help you stay grounded in what matters most, so you don't get swept away by exciting (but potentially misaligned) opportunities.

2. Research Their Track Record

Look into the other company's history and reputation. Have they consistently aligned their actions with their mission? Do they have a track record of social or environmental impact? Check out their website, social media, press releases, and customer reviews to get a sense of their brand and commitment to impact.

Example: Evaluating a Partnership with Fair Trade Brands

Imagine you're a fair-trade coffee brand looking to partner with a larger distribution company to reach more customers. Before jumping in, you'd want to check if this company has a history of supporting fair trade or ethical sourcing. If they've been criticized for poor labor practices, it's a red flag that their values might not match yours. On the other hand, if they've made positive strides in social impact, it's a sign that they're serious about mission alignment.

3. Assess Compatibility in Decision-Making and Goals

Once you've confirmed that the company's mission aligns with yours, it's time to dig into the details. Are you on the same page when it comes to long-term goals and decision-making processes? During your discussions, ask questions like:

- How do they make key decisions? Is profit always the top priority, or is mission just as important?
- How do they define success? Are they committed to measurable impact or just bottom-line growth?
- What are their plans for the future? Do they align with your vision?

Anecdote: Mission Misalignment and Lessons Learned

I once consulted for a nonprofit that partnered with a local company to host eco-friendly events. On the surface, it seemed like a good fit, as both were committed to environmental causes. But once they started working together, it became clear that the company prioritized cost-cutting over sustainability, frequently opting for cheaper, less eco-friendly materials. The partnership quickly fell apart, and it became a valuable lesson for the nonprofit about the importance of evaluating values beyond surface-level missions.

4. Look for Complementary Strengths

Mission alignment doesn't mean both businesses have to be identical. In fact, complementary strengths often make for the best partnerships. Look for partners who can fill in gaps in your resources or expertise, and vice versa. If you're great at product development but lack a strong marketing presence, for instance, look for a partner who can amplify your message.

Case Study: Beyond Meat and Fast Food Partnerships

Beyond Meat, the plant-based meat company, has partnered with fast-food giants like McDonald's, Dunkin', and KFC. While fast food might not immediately scream "mission alignment," these partnerships allow Beyond Meat to make plant-based eating accessible to more people, advancing its goal of reducing meat consumption and supporting the environment. The fast-food chains benefit from meeting the rising demand for plant-based options, creating a partnership that brings value to both parties.

Structuring Impactful Partnerships

Once you've found a compatible partner, the next step is to structure the partnership in a way that maximizes impact. This goes beyond signing a contract; it's about setting clear expectations, defining roles, and ensuring that both parties are committed to the shared mission. Here are some strategies for structuring partnerships that truly work.

1. Establish Clear, Shared Goals

Setting shared goals is essential to making sure both parties are working toward the same vision. These goals should be specific, measurable, and tied directly to your impact mission. For example, if you're partnering to distribute eco-friendly products, one goal might be to reach a certain number of new customers within a year, or to reduce plastic waste by a specific amount.

Tip: Define Both Impact Goals and Business Goals

In partnerships, it's important to balance impact goals with business goals. Agree on the impact you want to achieve—like reducing carbon emissions or supporting fair wages—while also setting targets for revenue or growth. Having both types of goals creates accountability and helps ensure that the partnership remains mutually beneficial.

2. Define Roles and Responsibilities

Successful partnerships require clear roles and responsibilities. This doesn't just mean dividing tasks; it means defining who will handle decision-making, reporting, and communication. Who's in charge of what? Make sure both parties are clear on their roles and comfortable with their responsibilities.

Anecdote: The Importance of Role Clarity in a Community Garden Project

In a community garden partnership I once worked on, two organizations joined forces: one provided the land, and the other offered resources like seeds, soil, and tools. At first, roles were vague, and tasks overlapped, causing confusion. Eventually, they clarified roles, with one organization managing the garden's day-to-day operations and the other focusing on community outreach. This clarity transformed the project, allowing each partner to play to their strengths and work more efficiently.

3. Build Accountability and Transparency

Trust is the foundation of any partnership, and trust is built through accountability and transparency. Agree on regular check-ins to discuss progress, review impact metrics, and address any challenges. By staying open about successes and setbacks, you're more likely to maintain a strong, productive partnership.

Example: Transparency in Warby Parker and VisionSpring's Partnership

Warby Parker partners with VisionSpring, a nonprofit that provides affordable eyewear to low-income communities. Both organizations maintain transparency by sharing data on how many glasses they distribute, the impact on local communities, and the outcomes for people's livelihoods. This transparency helps them stay accountable to their shared mission of providing eye care access and building trust with their supporters.

4. Create an Exit Plan

Even the best partnerships sometimes come to an end, and that's okay. Having an exit plan doesn't mean you're expecting failure; it's simply about being prepared. Outline conditions for ending the partnership and agree on how you'll handle shared resources or intellectual property if one party decides to move on. This foresight helps avoid conflicts and ensures a smooth transition if things change.

Tip: Use a "Sunset Clause" for Limited Partnerships

For partnerships that have a specific goal or timeline, consider using a "sunset clause," which sets an end date for the partnership. This gives both parties a natural point to evaluate whether to renew or part ways. It's a great way to keep things focused and avoid any lingering commitments.

Bringing It All Together

Acquiring or partnering with an aligned business can be a powerful way to scale your impact, but it requires careful planning and commitment to your mission. By choosing partners who share your values, setting clear goals, and maintaining open communication, you'll be better positioned to create a successful and impactful partnership.

Remember, the right partner can help you reach new heights and make a bigger difference than you ever could alone. With aligned goals, complementary strengths, and a shared commitment to impact, your social enterprise can thrive and expand in ways you never imagined. Whether it's through a strategic acquisition or a simple partnership, collaboration is one of the most effective ways to build a business that changes the world.

Part 3

Financing Impact-Driven Ventures

CHAPTER 8

Funding Options for Social Enterprises

Funding is the fuel that helps any business get off the ground, but for social enterprises, securing financial support is about more than just finding investors—it's about finding *the right* investors. You need people who believe in your mission, understand your goals, and are excited about helping you create positive change.

In this chapter, we're going to look at the different funding avenues for social enterprises, from impact investing and venture capital to angel investors and crowdfunding. We'll talk about how to craft pitches that appeal to purpose-driven investors, and we'll dive into strategies for using crowdfunding to rally community support and build momentum. Ready to learn how to finance your impact-driven venture? Let's get started!

A Breakdown of Impact Investment Types

When it comes to funding a social enterprise, it's essential to understand the variety of options available. Unlike traditional businesses, social enterprises benefit from funding sources that prioritize both financial returns and social impact. Let's explore some of the most popular impact investment options, each with its unique approach and benefits.

1. Impact Investing

Impact investing is a growing field that focuses on investments made with the intention of generating measurable social or environmental impact alongside a financial return. Impact investors are looking for more than profits; they want to see tangible, positive outcomes from the businesses they support. This funding type is perfect for social enterprises with a clear, measurable impact, as impact investors want to know their money is being put to good use.

Case Study: Acumen Fund's Support for Solar Entrepreneurs

Acumen, a pioneering impact investment fund, invests in early-stage companies tackling social issues in sectors like energy, health, and agriculture. One of Acumen's investments was in a solar energy company providing affordable, off-grid lighting solutions to communities without access to electricity. This not only improved the quality of life for people in these regions but also created job opportunities and supported sustainable development. By focusing on social and environmental benefits, Acumen's impact investments have fueled ventures that bring critical solutions to underserved communities.

Tip: If you're seeking impact investors, make sure your social and environmental metrics are clearly defined. Impact investors want to see both a business plan and a well-documented plan for tracking your impact over time.

2. Venture Capital (VC) with a Purpose

Traditional venture capital is focused on high-growth potential and returns, but there's a new wave of VCs committed to funding purpose-driven businesses. These VCs, often called "social venture funds" or "impact VCs," specifically look for businesses that combine profit with social or environmental goals. If your social enterprise is in a field with strong growth potential—like clean energy, ethical fashion, or health tech—this type of funding could be a good fit.

Example: DBL Partners and Their Support for Social Enterprises

DBL Partners is a VC firm that focuses on "Double Bottom Line" returns, meaning they're as interested in social impact as they are in financial gains. DBL Partners invested in Tesla when it was just a startup, recognizing not only the potential for growth but also the environmental impact of an electric car company. They've also backed companies in areas like sustainable food and affordable healthcare, helping these ventures grow while staying true to their missions.

3. Angel Investors with a Social Conscience

Angel investors are typically high-net-worth individuals who provide funding in exchange for equity in early-stage companies. In recent years, more angel investors have started looking for opportunities that offer social returns as well as financial ones. These mission-aligned angels often take a personal interest in the businesses they support and are willing to offer mentorship and connections in addition to financial backing.

Anecdote: A Social Enterprise's Success with an Angel Investor

A friend of mine started a sustainable packaging company with a mission to reduce plastic waste. She met an angel investor at a networking event who happened to be passionate about environmental issues. This investor not only provided her with the capital she needed to get her business off the ground but also connected her with other eco-conscious business leaders, helping her grow her network and scale her impact. For social entrepreneurs, finding an angel who shares your passion can be as valuable as the funding itself.

4. Crowdfunding: Funding with Community Support

Crowdfunding has become one of the most accessible ways to raise money for social enterprises. Platforms like Kickstarter, Indiegogo, and GoFundMe allow you to reach a large audience of potential supporters, and many of these platforms are designed specifically for social or environmental projects. Crowdfunding is ideal for early-stage funding, especially if you're creating a product or service that resonates with a wide audience.

Example: Who Gives a Crap's Crowdfunding Success

Who Gives a Crap, a toilet paper company that donates half its profits to building toilets in underserved areas, started with a crowdfunding campaign. The founders launched their campaign on Indiegogo, and they made it fun and engaging, even offering a live-streamed "sit-in" where the founder sat on a toilet until they reached their funding goal. The campaign went viral, raising enough money to kickstart the business and laying the groundwork for its loyal customer base. Today, Who Gives a Crap is a thriving social enterprise, thanks to the initial community support from crowdfunding.

Securing Impact-Driven Investors

Finding investors who care about impact as much as profits can be a challenge, but it's worth the effort. Impact-driven investors understand that a purpose-driven business might not always grow at the same rate as a traditional company. They're also more likely to be patient and supportive, understanding that meaningful change takes time. Here are some strategies for attracting these investors.

1. Tell a Story That Resonates

For impact-driven investors, numbers are important, but the story behind your business is just as vital. They want to know *why* you're passionate about your mission and *how* your work is making a difference. Create a narrative that connects with their values and shows them why they should care.

Anecdote: How an Entrepreneur Used Storytelling to Secure Funding

I once worked with a social entrepreneur who was building a company focused on providing clean water to remote villages. During her pitch, she didn't start with statistics or financial projections; she started with a story about her experience visiting a village that lacked clean water and witnessing the daily struggles of the community. This emotional connection resonated with the investors, who were immediately engaged. By the time she shared her business plan, they were already sold on the importance of her mission.

Tip: When pitching to impact-driven investors, remember that storytelling is about authenticity. Share your personal journey, the problem you're tackling, and the real-life impact of your work. Show them the *human* side of your business.

2. Highlight Both Social and Financial Returns

While impact-driven investors care about your mission, they also want to know that their investment is in good hands. Be transparent about your financial goals and demonstrate how you plan to achieve them. Show them that your business is both impactful and sustainable.

Example: Presenting a Double Bottom Line

Imagine you're pitching a social enterprise that provides affordable housing solutions. Start by highlighting the social impact —how your work will improve lives, reduce homelessness, and strengthen communities. Then, transition to the financial side: show them the revenue model, projected growth, and potential return on investment. By clearly presenting both social and financial returns, you'll show investors that your business is built for sustainability.

3. Show Your Impact Metrics

Impact-driven investors are often data-driven. They want to see that you're not just talking about impact but actually measuring it. Share specific metrics and outcomes to demonstrate your business's success in achieving its mission.

Tip: Use Metrics that Matter to Investors**

Metrics might include the number of people served, percentage reduction in waste, lives improved, or carbon emissions reduced. For example, if you run an educational nonprofit, you could measure the number of students reached, graduation rates, or improvement in test scores. The more specific you can be, the more credibility you'll have with investors.

4. Find the Right Investor Networks

Impact-driven investors aren't always easy to find, but several networks and organizations can help you connect with like-minded funders. Look for impact investment networks, pitch competitions, and conferences focused on social entrepreneurship.

Example: Social Capital Markets (SOCAP) Conference

SOCAP is a yearly conference where impact investors, social entrepreneurs, and changemakers come together to discuss the future of social impact. Many social enterprises have secured funding simply by attending SOCAP, meeting investors who are passionate about their mission. Events like SOCAP can be a great way to find investors who are aligned with your goals.

Crowdfunding for Purpose-Driven Projects

Crowdfunding has transformed the way social enterprises can raise money, offering a democratic, community-based funding model. It's especially helpful for early-stage ventures or projects that may not attract traditional investors right away. Crowdfunding isn't just about raising money; it's also a chance to build community support and market your business. Here's how to make the most of it.

1. Choose the Right Platform

Different platforms cater to different types of projects. For social enterprises, some of the best options include:

- **Kickstarter**: Great for creative products or innovative ideas. Kickstarter campaigns are all-or-nothing, so you must reach your funding goal to receive any funds.
- **Indiegogo**: Offers flexible funding options, meaning you can keep what you raise even if you don't reach your goal. This is ideal for social ventures with ongoing funding needs.
- **StartSomeGood**: Specifically designed for social enterprises and nonprofits, StartSomeGood attracts a community of impact-minded supporters.
- **Patreon**: Useful for creators or educators who want to build a community of monthly supporters. This works well for businesses that offer continuous content or updates.

Example: A Crowdfunding Platform Success

The makers of the solar-powered water bottle, SolarPuff, used Kickstarter to raise funds for their product, designed to provide portable light to communities without electricity. Their campaign raised more than double their initial goal, allowing them to distribute SolarPuffs to communities in need and build a loyal customer base.

2. Create an Engaging Campaign Video

A campaign video is often the first thing people see when they visit your crowdfunding page. It's a chance to tell your story, explain your mission, and get people excited about your project. The video doesn't have to be a Hollywood production, but it should be clear, heartfelt, and compelling.

Anecdote: How One Social Entrepreneur Hooked Backers with a

Simple Video

I once helped a social entrepreneur create a video for her sustainable fashion brand's Kickstarter. She didn't have a big budget, so we kept it simple. She filmed herself in her workshop, talking about her passion for eco-friendly clothing and her vision for a more sustainable fashion industry. Her authenticity shone through, and the campaign quickly gained traction, surpassing her goal within a few days. Sometimes, simplicity and sincerity are all you need to connect with people.

3. Offer Creative Rewards

Rewards are a key part of crowdfunding. Think about what you can offer backers that's both meaningful and aligned with your mission. Rewards could include early access to products, branded merchandise, or even virtual "thank you" notes that show your appreciation.

Tip: Tailor Rewards to Different Levels**

For example, offer a small token for a $10 pledge, a product for a $50 pledge, and a unique experience—like a behind-the-scenes tour or a video call with the founders—for larger pledges. Make sure each reward feels like a part of your mission.

4. Engage Your Community

Successful crowdfunding campaigns don't happen overnight; they're fueled by community engagement. Update your backers regularly, share your campaign on social media, and encourage friends, family, and supporters to spread the word.

Example: Engaging Supporters with Social Media

A sustainable skincare brand I worked with ran a crowdfunding campaign and used Instagram to build excitement. They posted stories and behind-the-scenes videos daily, sharing updates, milestones, and even setbacks. Their followers felt like part of the journey, which boosted engagement and ultimately led to a successful campaign.

Bringing It All Together

Funding a social enterprise requires creativity, persistence, and an understanding of the different types of investors and supporters out there. From impact investing and venture capital to angel investors and crowdfunding, each funding source offers unique benefits and challenges.

Remember, the key to securing funding isn't just about finding investors or backers—it's about building relationships with people who share your vision. By telling a compelling story, showcasing both social and financial returns, and engaging your community, you'll be well on your way to raising the capital you need to grow your impact-driven venture.

Your journey is about more than raising money. It's about building a movement, creating a community of supporters, and making a difference, one investment at a time. So, go out there, share your vision, and let the world know how they can be part of something truly impactful.

CHAPTER 9

Accessing Grants and Strategic Resources

Finding the right resources can make all the difference when building a social enterprise. While many for-profit businesses focus on investors, loans, and revenue streams, social enterprises have a unique advantage—they're often eligible for grants and support from foundations, governments, and nonprofit organizations that prioritize social impact.

In this chapter, we'll dive into the world of grants and strategic resources, covering everything from where to find funding, how to craft a winning application, and how to build partnerships with organizations that can help amplify your impact. Ready to learn how to secure resources that can fuel your mission? Let's get started!

Finding Grants for Social Ventures

Grants can be a lifeline for social enterprises, providing much-needed capital without the pressure of repayment or profit-sharing. Unlike traditional loans or investment funds, grants allow you to focus on impact rather than just financial returns. But here's the catch: finding the right grants can feel like looking for a needle in a haystack, especially if you're new to the world of social impact funding. Let's break down some of the best places to find grants for social ventures.

1. Start with Foundations and Philanthropic Organizations

Many foundations and philanthropic organizations have specific programs to support social entrepreneurs, especially those tackling pressing social issues like poverty, education, health, and the environment. Here are a few well-known foundations to consider:

- **Ford Foundation**: Supports social justice, economic opportunity, and sustainability initiatives.
- **Bill & Melinda Gates Foundation**: Focuses on global health, education, and economic empowerment, particularly in underserved communities.
- **Skoll Foundation**: Supports social entrepreneurs working on scalable solutions to global challenges.

Case Study: Skoll Foundation's Support for Social Entrepreneurs

The Skoll Foundation has been a significant funder of social enterprises, awarding millions to ventures that focus on issues like clean energy, poverty reduction, and access to healthcare. One Skoll grantee, One Acre Fund, provides loans, seeds, and training to smallholder farmers in Africa, helping them increase their crop yields and improve their families' lives. With the Skoll Foundation's support, One Acre Fund scaled its model and expanded to new countries, reaching hundreds of thousands of farmers and creating a massive impact.

Tip: Each foundation has its own priorities, so be sure to research their focus areas carefully. Many foundations are very specific about the kinds of social issues they support, and aligning your mission with their goals can significantly increase your chances of securing funding.

2. Explore Government Grants and Public Funding Programs

Governments worldwide offer grants and funding programs for social enterprises, particularly those that address local or national priorities like job creation, environmental protection, and public health. In the U.S., for example, agencies like the Small Business

Administration (SBA), the Department of Health and Human Services, and the Department of Energy offer grants for mission-driven businesses. The European Union also has several funding programs, including Horizon Europe, for social impact initiatives.

Example: The Small Business Innovation Research (SBIR) Program

The SBIR program provides funding for U.S. small businesses engaged in innovative projects that support national priorities, from renewable energy to public health. Through this program, social enterprises can receive funding in the form of grants or contracts to develop solutions that benefit society. For example, a startup developing affordable solar technology could receive SBIR funding to support research and development, allowing them to make a greater impact on sustainable energy access.

Tip: Government grants can be competitive and often have strict eligibility requirements. Before applying, read the guidelines carefully and ensure your social enterprise aligns with the program's goals. Government grants also tend to have detailed reporting requirements, so be prepared to track and report on your progress if awarded.

3. Use Grant Databases and Online Platforms

For social entrepreneurs, finding grants doesn't have to be a solo journey. There are many online platforms that aggregate grants for social ventures, making it easier to find funding opportunities tailored to your mission. Here are a few popular options:

- **GrantStation**: Provides a database of grant opportunities for nonprofits, social enterprises, and community projects.
- **Candid (formerly Foundation Center)**: Offers access to a database of thousands of foundations and grants. The subscription-based service, Foundation Directory Online, is highly regarded in the nonprofit sector.

- **Grants.gov**: Lists government grants in the U.S., including those focused on social impact, health, and sustainability.

Anecdote: How an Entrepreneur Found Funding on GrantStation

I once worked with a social entrepreneur who started a project focused on reducing food waste. After struggling to find funding, she signed up for GrantStation and discovered a grant from a foundation interested in supporting environmental sustainability projects. She applied, received the grant, and was able to launch a program that diverted hundreds of tons of food waste from landfills. Sometimes, the right resource is just a click away!

Tip: Many grant databases offer free trials or affordable monthly rates. If you're new to grant-seeking, try one out and see if it's a good fit. You might just find a funding source you wouldn't have discovered otherwise.

Applying for and Winning Grants

Finding the right grant is only half the battle—the other half is crafting a compelling application. Grant applications can be competitive, so it's essential to create an application that stands out and clearly aligns with the funder's goals. Here are some strategies to increase your chances of winning grants for your social enterprise.

1. Understand the Funder's Mission and Goals

Every grant-giving organization has specific objectives they're trying to achieve, and your application should show that your mission aligns with theirs. Take the time to research the funder's priorities, read past grant recipients' stories, and review any application guidelines they provide. This background research can help you tailor your application to address their specific interests.

Example: Crafting a Mission-Driven Application

Imagine you're applying for a grant from a foundation focused on poverty reduction. Instead of simply describing your social enterprise as a job-training program, emphasize how your program directly addresses poverty by providing job skills, creating economic opportunities, and reducing unemployment in underserved communities. Highlight the outcomes you've achieved, like the number of people employed or the increase in income for participants. Tailoring your application in this way shows that you understand the funder's goals and that your mission is closely aligned with theirs.

Tip: Use the funder's language and terms when possible. Many foundations have specific words or phrases they use to describe their priorities. Incorporating these terms into your application shows that you've done your research and understand their focus areas.

2. Be Specific and Quantify Your Impact

One of the most common mistakes in grant applications is being too vague. Funders want to know exactly how their money will be used and the impact it will create. Be as specific as possible in describing your project, your goals, and the outcomes you expect.

Anecdote: An Entrepreneur Who Quantified Her Impact

A friend of mine applied for a grant to support a social enterprise that provides affordable tutoring for students from low-income families. Instead of saying, "We help students improve their academic performance," she quantified her impact: "Last year, 85% of our students improved their grades by at least one letter within six months." By providing specific data, she demonstrated the effectiveness of her program and made it easier for the funder to see the value of her work.

3. Tell a Compelling Story

While data is essential, it's also important to tell a story that captures the funder's heart. Share a personal story or example that illustrates the problem you're solving and the impact you're making. This narrative helps bring your application to life and makes it memorable.

Tip: Use a success story to illustrate your impact. For example, if your social enterprise helps women start small businesses, include a short story about one of the women you've supported and how her life has changed because of your program. Personal stories make your application more relatable and emotionally engaging.

4. Outline a Clear and Realistic Budget

Funders want to see that you're using their money wisely, so a clear, realistic budget is a must. Break down your expenses in detail and show exactly how the grant will be used to further your mission. Be transparent and realistic, and avoid inflating your costs.

Example: Budget Breakdown for a Youth Education Program

Imagine you're applying for a grant to support a youth education program. Instead of saying, "We need $50,000 for program expenses," provide a detailed budget. For example:

- $15,000 for educational materials and supplies
- $20,000 for staff salaries and training
- $10,000 for facility rental and utilities
- $5,000 for transportation and outreach

This transparency shows funders that you've carefully planned your project and that you understand how to allocate resources effectively.

Leveraging Nonprofit Support Organizations

In addition to grants, social enterprises can benefit from partnerships with nonprofit support organizations and government agencies. These organizations provide more than just funding—they offer networks, resources, training, and credibility, all of which can amplify your impact. Let's explore how to make the most of these strategic partnerships.

1. Partner with Nonprofits for Mutual Support

Nonprofits are often more than willing to collaborate with social enterprises that share their mission. Partnerships with nonprofits can help you access new networks, connect with potential customers or beneficiaries, and even gain access to resources like office space, training, and volunteers.

Example: Social Enterprise and Nonprofit Collaboration

A social enterprise focused on providing affordable medical equipment partnered with a health-focused nonprofit to expand its reach. The nonprofit had connections with clinics and hospitals, allowing the social enterprise to get its products into the hands of people who needed them. In return, the nonprofit benefited from the social enterprise's expertise and innovative solutions. This partnership helped both organizations amplify their impact and reach more people.

2. Explore Government-Supported Resources for Small Businesses

Many government agencies offer programs designed to support small businesses and social enterprises. For example, the Small Business Administration (SBA) provides mentorship, training, and access to loan programs. Agencies focused on economic development, labor, or the environment may also offer resources and funding for mission-driven businesses.

Anecdote: How an Environmental Social Enterprise Used Government Support

A social enterprise dedicated to reducing plastic waste partnered with a state environmental agency that provided funding and technical support. The agency helped the enterprise implement a recycling program, and in return, the agency benefited from data and insights that helped them in their broader environmental efforts. By leveraging this government partnership, the social enterprise scaled its program more quickly than it could have on its own.

3. Tap Into Business Accelerators for Social Ventures

Social enterprise accelerators are programs designed to help mission-driven businesses grow. Many accelerators provide funding, mentorship, and connections to impact investors, making them an excellent resource for social entrepreneurs. Look for accelerators that focus on social impact, such as the Unreasonable Institute, Echoing Green, and Village Capital.

Example: Village Capital's Social Enterprise Accelerator

Village Capital runs an accelerator that connects social enterprises with mentors, resources, and investors. Social entrepreneurs who participate in Village Capital's program receive mentorship, networking opportunities, and even the chance to secure funding. Many graduates go on to scale their ventures and make significant social impacts, thanks to the support they received from the accelerator.

4. Join Industry-Specific Networks

Industry-specific networks and associations are another valuable resource for social entrepreneurs. Many of these networks provide access to funding, training, and conferences, allowing you to stay connected with others in your field and learn best practices.

Tip: Look for networks relevant to your industry. For example, if your social enterprise focuses on renewable energy, join an organization like the Solar Energy Industries Association (SEIA). If you're in sustainable fashion, consider groups like the Sustainable Apparel Coalition. These networks can provide targeted support, industry insights, and valuable connections.

Bringing It All Together

Securing grants and strategic resources requires a combination of research, careful planning, and relationship-building. From finding the right grants and crafting compelling applications to forming partnerships with nonprofits and government agencies, there's a wealth of support available for social enterprises willing to seek it out.

Remember, building a social enterprise isn't just about having the right funding—it's about aligning with people and organizations that share your vision for impact. By tapping into grants, leveraging strategic partnerships, and maximizing support from nonprofit and government organizations, you'll be better equipped to create a sustainable and impactful venture that can truly make a difference.

Your mission is bigger than just one business. With the right resources, partnerships, and planning, you can build something that has a lasting impact on the world. So go out there, find your allies, and get the support you need to turn your vision into reality.

Part 4
Building, Branding, and Growing Impact

CHAPTER 10

Creating a Purpose-Driven Brand

Building a social enterprise is about more than delivering a product or service—it's about creating a brand that people believe in. When you're focused on a mission, your brand becomes a bridge between your business and the impact you're trying to create. And here's the magic: people want to feel like they're part of something meaningful, so when they connect with your brand's purpose, they're not just buying a product; they're investing in a movement.

In this chapter, we're going to explore how to develop a brand identity that's rooted in your mission, how to use storytelling to engage audiences emotionally, and ways to leverage social media and digital marketing to promote your brand's purpose. Let's dive into creating a brand that not only stands out but also stands for something.

Developing a Brand Identity around Mission

Creating a purpose-driven brand means embedding your mission into every part of your identity. Your brand should be an authentic reflection of your core values, and it should resonate with people who care about the same issues you do. Let's break down what it takes to develop a brand identity that's as impactful as it is memorable.

1. Define Your Brand's Core Values

Before you even think about logos, colors, or taglines, start with your values. These are the principles that drive your business, the beliefs that keep you and your team motivated, and the standards that define how you want to operate. Your values will act as a compass for every decision you make.

Tip: Choose Values That Align with Your Audience

Your brand's values should resonate with your audience. Think about what they care about and choose values that reflect shared priorities. For instance, if your social enterprise focuses on sustainable fashion, your values might include transparency, ethical production, and environmental responsibility. If you're working in education, your values might include accessibility, empowerment, and lifelong learning.

Example: Patagonia's Core Values

Patagonia is known for its dedication to environmental activism, and it's woven this commitment into every aspect of its brand. From sustainable sourcing to supporting grassroots environmental organizations, Patagonia's values of sustainability, responsibility, and transparency shine through. This strong sense of purpose has attracted a loyal following of customers who share these values and want to support a company that's walking the talk.

2. Craft Your Brand Message

Your brand message is the heartbeat of your identity. It's a simple, compelling statement that explains what you do, why it matters, and how it aligns with your mission. A great brand message captures your purpose in a way that's both clear and emotionally resonant, making it easy for people to understand and connect with your vision.

Anecdote: A Small Social Enterprise Finds Its Voice

A friend of mine started a small social enterprise focused on reducing plastic waste by selling reusable kitchen products. At first, her messaging was all over the place—she was trying to talk about product quality, environmental impact, and lifestyle benefits all at once. But after digging deeper, she simplified her message to this: "Helping you live sustainably, one choice at a time." It was simple, direct, and instantly communicated her mission. As soon as she updated her messaging, she noticed that customers were more engaged and supportive because they understood the purpose behind the brand.

Tip: Keep your message simple. It should be something people can remember and share easily. Ask yourself, "If I had only 10 seconds to explain my brand, what would I say?"

3. Use Visuals to Reflect Your Mission

Visuals are a powerful way to communicate your brand's purpose. Your logo, colors, fonts, and imagery should all reflect your mission and values. If you're a sustainability-focused brand, you might choose earthy tones and natural imagery. If you're focused on education, you might use clear, approachable fonts and bright, optimistic colors.

Example: Who Gives a Crap's Playful Branding

Who Gives a Crap, the eco-friendly toilet paper company, uses playful and vibrant visuals that reflect their lighthearted approach to a serious mission: improving sanitation and reducing waste. Their logo is simple and fun, their colors are bright, and their product packaging is as eco-friendly as their mission. Their branding shows that you can tackle important issues without taking yourself too seriously, which has helped them connect with customers who care about both sustainability and humor.

Tip: Think about what feelings you want your brand to evoke. Should it feel bold and activist-driven? Warm and supportive? Fun and approachable? Let these feelings guide your visual choices.

Storytelling for Impact

Storytelling is one of the most powerful tools a purpose-driven brand can use. When you tell a story, you're not just sharing facts or features—you're inviting people to experience your mission, to understand the "why" behind what you do. Here's how to make storytelling a central part of your brand's impact.

1. Share the "Why" Behind Your Brand

People want to know what inspired you to start your social enterprise. Was there a personal experience that ignited your passion? A problem you witnessed firsthand? Sharing this origin story makes your mission more relatable and helps people feel emotionally invested in your journey.

Anecdote: TOMS Shoes and the Power of Origin Stories

TOMS Shoes founder Blake Mycoskie famously launched the brand after a trip to Argentina, where he saw children who didn't have shoes. His experience sparked the idea for a company that would provide shoes for every pair sold. By sharing this story, TOMS created a direct emotional connection with its customers, allowing them to feel like they were part of the mission every time they bought a pair of shoes. The "why" behind TOMS' brand has become its core identity, showing how powerful a story can be in building a brand with impact.

Tip: Reflect on your own journey and why you felt compelled to start your social enterprise. Share this story on your website, in social media posts, and in your marketing materials. Make your "why" a central part of your brand.

2. Highlight Stories of Impact

As you grow, collect stories from the people or communities you're impacting. These stories add depth to your mission, showing that your work is making a real difference. Feature them on your website, in newsletters, or in videos that you share with your audience. When people can see the direct impact of your work, they're more likely to feel a sense of connection and purpose.

Example: Warby Parker's Vision Impact Stories

Warby Parker, known for its "Buy a Pair, Give a Pair" model, often shares stories about the people who benefit from their donations. By highlighting how each pair of donated glasses has changed lives—enabling people to work, study, and connect with the world—Warby Parker makes its mission tangible. These impact stories allow customers to see the direct result of their purchase and feel a sense of pride in supporting a meaningful cause.

Tip: If possible, ask for testimonials from people you've helped or from customers who believe in your mission. These personal accounts can be incredibly powerful in showing the real-world impact of your work.

3. Show Your Challenges and Growth

People love to root for a brand that's authentic, and one of the best ways to show authenticity is by sharing both your successes and challenges. Don't be afraid to let people in on the hurdles you're facing or the lessons you're learning along the way. Being open about your journey makes your brand relatable and shows that you're committed to continuous growth.

Anecdote: A Local Nonprofit Shares Its Struggles

A local nonprofit that supports low-income families with meal delivery started sharing some of the challenges it faced on social media, like rising food costs and volunteer shortages. They didn't hide the struggle; instead, they used it as an opportunity to rally community support. People were moved by their transparency and donated both time and money, which helped the nonprofit continue its mission. By being open, they strengthened their community's connection to their cause.

Tip: Use social media to share behind-the-scenes updates, lessons learned, and honest reflections on your journey. People appreciate authenticity, and it builds trust.

Social Media and Digital Marketing Strategies

Social media and digital marketing can amplify your brand's message, allowing you to reach people who care about your mission and want to support your work. But it's not just about posting regularly; it's about building relationships and creating a sense of community around your purpose. Here are some strategies for using digital platforms to promote transparency, accountability, and social responsibility.

1. Be Transparent About Your Mission and Practices

Transparency is essential for purpose-driven brands. People want to know not only what you're doing but also how you're doing it. Share details about your sourcing, your production methods, and your impact metrics. When people see that you're committed to accountability, they're more likely to trust and support your brand.

Example: Everlane's "Radical Transparency" Approach

Everlane, a sustainable fashion brand, has built its brand on a commitment to "radical transparency." They share detailed information about their factories, pricing breakdowns, and materials. By showing customers exactly where their money goes and how their products are made, Everlane has built a loyal following of consumers who value ethical production. This transparency has become one of Everlane's biggest assets, setting them apart in a crowded market.

Tip: Create a "Transparency" or "Impact" page on your website where you share information about your practices. Update it regularly with new insights and metrics, showing customers that you're dedicated to honesty and accountability.

2. Use Social Media to Highlight Social Responsibility

Social media platforms offer the perfect space to show your audience that you're socially responsible. Highlight the impact of your work, support causes that align with your values, and use your voice to advocate for change. Social media is where you can rally your community, raise awareness, and create conversations around important issues.

Anecdote: How One Business Uses Instagram for Advocacy

A small fair-trade coffee company I know uses Instagram to share stories about the coffee farmers they work with. They post videos of farm visits, photos of the harvesting process, and captions that highlight the importance of fair wages. By using their platform to educate customers about ethical sourcing, they've built a loyal following of people who value fair-trade practices. Their Instagram isn't just about selling coffee; it's about promoting a cause.

Tip: Use your social media to amplify not only your brand but also the causes you believe in. Share statistics, facts, and stories that educate and inspire action.

3. Engage Your Audience with Interactive Content

One of the best ways to build a community around your brand is by engaging your audience in meaningful ways. Create interactive content that invites people to participate, whether it's through polls, Q&As, or challenges. Give your followers a chance to be part of your mission and celebrate their involvement.

Example: A Challenge to Reduce Plastic Use

A sustainable product company once launched a "Plastic-Free Challenge" on social media, encouraging followers to reduce their plastic consumption for a week. They shared daily tips and resources, and followers posted their own progress using a branded hashtag. This challenge not only created engagement but also strengthened the brand's mission and gave followers a direct way to participate in the cause.

Tip: Think of fun, interactive ways to get people involved in your mission. Encourage them to share their experiences, and celebrate their participation. This builds a sense of community and makes them feel like active contributors to your brand's purpose.

Bringing It All Together

Creating a purpose-driven brand is about much more than marketing—it's about building a movement that people want to be part of. By developing an identity rooted in your mission, telling stories that connect emotionally, and using digital platforms to promote your values, you'll create a brand that not only attracts customers but also inspires them.

Remember, your brand is a reflection of who you are, what you stand for, and the impact you're committed to making. Embrace authenticity, transparency, and engagement as you build, and watch as your brand becomes a beacon for people who want to make a difference.

Your journey isn't just about selling a product or service—it's about leading a community toward a better, brighter future. So, go out there, share your story, and let your brand become a force for good.

CHAPTER 11

Measuring and Reporting Impact

Building a social enterprise is more than just saying you want to make a difference—it's about proving it. For people to believe in your mission, they need to see evidence that you're genuinely creating positive change. And the best way to do that? Measure your impact, report it transparently, and use the data to continually improve. Measuring impact isn't just about satisfying investors or customers; it's about holding yourself accountable and making sure your business is truly achieving what you set out to do.

In this chapter, we'll guide you through selecting the right impact metrics, share tips for transparent reporting, and show how data can be a powerful tool for growth and improvement. Let's dive in!

Selecting Impact Metrics

When it comes to impact, one size doesn't fit all. Every social enterprise has unique goals, communities they serve, and challenges they're addressing. The key is choosing metrics that genuinely reflect your mission and show the difference you're making. Metrics can be overwhelming, so start with the basics and build from there.

1. Start with Your Mission and Objectives

The first step in selecting impact metrics is to revisit your mission. What's the core problem your business aims to solve? What specific change are you hoping to create? Your impact metrics should align closely with these objectives, providing measurable proof that you're making progress.

Example: A Social Enterprise Focused on Clean Water

Imagine your social enterprise provides clean drinking water to rural communities. Your primary mission is to improve access to safe water, so your impact metrics should directly reflect that. You might track metrics like the number of people with access to clean water, the reduction in waterborne illnesses, and the amount of water supplied to each community. These metrics connect directly to your mission, showing stakeholders exactly how you're making an impact.

Tip: Keep it simple. Start with three to five core metrics that best represent your mission. As you grow, you can expand to include additional indicators.

2. Choose Metrics That Matter to Your Stakeholders

Think about who's invested in your mission—customers, funders, community members—and consider what impact metrics matter most to them. If you're a sustainable fashion brand, for instance, customers may want to know about your environmental footprint, while investors might be more interested in your supply chain transparency and fair labor practices.

Anecdote: A Sustainable Skincare Brand's Metrics

A friend of mine runs a sustainable skincare company, and one of her brand promises is to reduce plastic waste. Knowing that her customers care about sustainability, she tracks metrics like the amount of plastic saved by using recycled packaging, the number of containers refilled by customers, and the percentage of biodegradable materials in her products. Her customers love seeing these numbers, and it's helped build loyalty and trust.

Tip: Ask for feedback. Survey your customers, investors, and partners to understand which impact metrics they find most valuable. This can give you direction and ensure you're sharing the data that matters most to them.

3. Utilize Tools and Frameworks for Impact Measurement

If you're new to impact measurement, it can help to use established tools and frameworks. Tools like IRIS+ and SDG-aligned indicators can give you a structured way to choose and track impact metrics that align with global standards.

- **IRIS+ (Impact Reporting and Investment Standards):** Developed by the Global Impact Investing Network, IRIS+ provides standardized metrics for social, environmental, and financial performance. It's an excellent resource for social enterprises looking for metrics that investors recognize and value.
- **SDG-Aligned Indicators:** The United Nations Sustainable Development Goals (SDGs) are a global framework for addressing social and environmental issues. Each SDG has specific indicators that can guide your metrics. For example, if your business focuses on clean energy, aligning your metrics with SDG 7 (Affordable and Clean Energy) shows how your work contributes to global goals.

Case Study: A Social Enterprise Using SDG Metrics

A social enterprise focused on education might align its metrics with SDG 4 (Quality Education). They could measure the number of students reached, improvements in literacy rates, and student satisfaction. By aligning with the SDGs, this business doesn't just show impact—they position themselves as part of a global effort, which appeals to stakeholders who value larger-scale impact.

Tip: Start small when using these frameworks. IRIS+ and the SDGs offer a wealth of metrics, so pick a few that best align with your mission and expand as you grow more comfortable with data collection.

Transparency and Reporting

Transparency in reporting builds trust. When you openly share your successes, challenges, and lessons learned, it shows that you're genuinely committed to your mission. Transparent reporting is essential for maintaining credibility with customers, investors, and communities who care about your impact.

1. Share Both Successes and Challenges

No social enterprise is perfect, and trying to appear that way can actually harm your credibility. People understand that change is difficult, so be open about the challenges you face. Whether it's supply chain issues, regulatory hurdles, or scaling difficulties, sharing these setbacks shows that you're committed to transparency and improvement.

Anecdote: A Fair-Trade Coffee Brand's Honest Report

A fair-trade coffee brand I know struggled with production issues after a crop failure affected their suppliers. Instead of hiding the problem, they were upfront with their customers, explaining the shortage and how they were working with farmers to address it. Customers appreciated the honesty, and it actually strengthened loyalty. By being transparent, the brand built trust and reinforced its commitment to ethical sourcing.

Tip: Acknowledge your challenges, but also share how you're addressing them. This transparency builds credibility and shows that you're focused on continuous improvement.

2. Choose Accessible and Engaging Formats

Impact reports don't have to be lengthy or filled with jargon. Think about your audience and choose formats that make your data accessible and engaging. This could be an annual report, an interactive webpage, or a series of social media updates. Visuals like infographics, charts, and videos can make complex data easy to understand and more memorable.

Example: Patagonia's Environmental Impact Report

Patagonia, known for its environmental activism, publishes an annual "Environmental & Social Responsibility" report. But they go beyond traditional reports, using infographics, videos, and personal stories to bring their data to life. This accessible format makes their impact clear and easy for consumers to understand, reinforcing their reputation as a purpose-driven brand.

Tip: Experiment with different formats to see what resonates best with your audience. Try a mix of visuals, storytelling, and data to make your impact report engaging.

3. Report Regularly and Consistently

Consistency is key in transparent reporting. Regular updates—whether quarterly, biannually, or annually—keep stakeholders informed and show that impact measurement is an ongoing priority. By reporting consistently, you create a sense of accountability that strengthens trust with your audience.

Example: A Nonprofit's Monthly Impact Update

A nonprofit I follow sends monthly impact updates via email. These updates are short and simple, focusing on one or two key metrics and sharing a success story or upcoming project. The consistency of these updates keeps supporters engaged and reinforces the nonprofit's commitment to transparency.

Tip: Don't feel pressured to produce a detailed report every month. Consistent, small updates can be just as effective in keeping your audience engaged and informed.

Using Data for Continuous Improvement

Data isn't just for sharing your impact—it's also a powerful tool for growth and refinement. By analyzing your impact data, you can identify areas for improvement, refine your strategy, and ensure you're always working toward greater effectiveness. Here's how to make data part of your ongoing improvement process.

1. Track Your Progress Over Time

Tracking your impact over time shows you whether you're truly making progress. Look for trends in your data to understand which strategies are working and where you might need to pivot. Are your metrics improving? Are you reaching more people or reducing waste as you grow? Use these insights to adjust your approach as needed.

Case Study: A Job Training Program's Data-Driven Adjustments

A job training program aimed at helping people re-enter the workforce was tracking metrics like job placement rates and retention. They noticed that placement rates were high, but retention rates dropped after three months. After digging deeper, they realized that many trainees lacked soft skills needed for long-term employment. In response, they added a soft-skills module to their program, which led to improved retention and more successful placements.

Tip: Use data as a diagnostic tool. When you spot trends—whether positive or negative—look for underlying causes and think about what adjustments could improve your impact.

2. Gather Qualitative Data for Deeper Insights

Numbers are valuable, but qualitative data—like feedback from beneficiaries, partners, or employees—adds depth to your understanding of impact. Collect stories, testimonials, and open-ended feedback to gain insights that numbers alone might not reveal. Qualitative data can help you understand the human side of your impact and refine your approach to meet people's needs more effectively.

Anecdote: Gathering Feedback from Community Members

A social enterprise focused on education was tracking test score improvements to measure its impact. But when they conducted focus groups with parents and students, they learned that emotional support and mentorship were equally important. Based on this feedback, they added mentorship components to their programs, which boosted not only test scores but also student satisfaction and engagement.

Tip: Use surveys, interviews, and focus groups to gather qualitative insights. Combine this feedback with your quantitative data to get a full picture of your impact.

3. Set Benchmarks and Goals for Growth

Once you have baseline data, use it to set realistic benchmarks and goals for growth. By establishing clear targets, you'll have a roadmap for what success looks like and a way to measure progress over time. These goals can be both short-term (like quarterly goals) and long-term (like annual or multi-year targets).

Example: Setting Benchmarks for a Clean Energy Initiative

A clean energy social enterprise set benchmarks to measure its progress in reducing carbon emissions. Their goals included reaching 10,000 households with solar energy within two years and reducing emissions by a specific amount. With these benchmarks in place, they could track their progress and demonstrate concrete outcomes to stakeholders.

Tip: Set "SMART" goals—Specific, Measurable, Achievable, Relevant, and Time-bound. SMART goals give you clear milestones to work toward and make it easier to measure and celebrate progress.

Bringing It All Together

Measuring and reporting impact is about more than tracking data; it's about creating a culture of accountability, transparency, and growth within your social enterprise. By selecting meaningful metrics, committing to honest reporting, and using data to continuously improve, you'll not only prove your impact but also strengthen your mission and build trust with your community.

Remember, impact measurement is an ongoing journey. Your metrics may evolve, your reporting formats may change, and your goals may shift as you grow. Embrace these changes as opportunities to refine your approach and deepen your impact.

Creating positive change is a long-term commitment, and every piece of data, every report, and every story you share brings you closer to that goal. So go out there, measure what matters, and let your impact speak for itself.

Part 5

Scaling for Greater Impact and Innovation

CHAPTER 12

Scaling Strategies for Social Enterprises

When it comes to scaling a social enterprise, growth isn't just about increasing revenue or expanding your customer base. Scaling an impact-driven business is about amplifying your mission and reaching more people without compromising your core values. As a social entrepreneur, your goal is not only to grow but to do so in a way that enhances, rather than dilutes, the positive impact you set out to create.

In this chapter, we'll explore strategies to grow sustainably, learn from social enterprises that have scaled successfully, and examine how digital tools can open new doors for impact. Whether you're at the beginning of your scaling journey or considering ways to expand even further, these insights will guide you in building a business that grows with purpose.

Scaling While Maintaining Mission

Scaling is exciting—it means your social enterprise is gaining traction, your audience is expanding, and the potential for impact is growing. But scaling can also bring pressure to compromise on values. To grow without mission drift, you need to approach expansion intentionally, setting clear priorities and boundaries. Here are some effective strategies to scale without losing sight of your purpose.

1. Strategic Partnerships

When scaling, partnerships can help you extend your reach, improve efficiency, and access new resources. By working with organizations that align with your values, you can grow your impact without straining your resources. Strategic partnerships allow you to tap into expertise, networks, and credibility that would otherwise take years to build on your own.

Example: Fair Trade USA's Partnership Model

Fair Trade USA certifies products to ensure they meet rigorous social and environmental standards. Rather than scaling independently, Fair Trade USA partners with companies across multiple industries, such as coffee, cocoa, and apparel, who commit to fair trade practices. These partnerships allow Fair Trade USA to expand its mission through trusted brands, reaching consumers who may never have considered fair trade products before. This model has enabled them to create significant impact without building out massive operational infrastructure on their own.

Tip: When choosing partners, look for organizations that share your values and audience. A good partnership is one where both parties' strengths complement each other and lead to greater collective impact.

2. Licensing Your Model

If you've created a proven, replicable model, licensing can be a fantastic way to scale impact without overstretching your resources. Licensing involves allowing others to replicate your business model or mission in new markets, often for a fee. By licensing your model, you can expand your mission into different regions while ensuring that your standards and values are maintained.

Case Study: Grameen Foundation's Microfinance Model

Grameen Foundation is known for pioneering the concept of microfinance—offering small loans to individuals in developing countries who wouldn't typically have access to traditional banking. As the model gained popularity, Grameen began licensing it to other organizations globally, from Africa to Latin America. By developing clear guidelines and providing ongoing support to licensees, Grameen has been able to scale its impact to multiple regions without taking on all the operational demands themselves.

Tip: Licensing requires a strong foundation, clear processes, and rigorous training for licensees. Create detailed guides and maintain ongoing support to ensure that your mission is consistently delivered.

3. Franchising with Purpose

Franchising allows you to scale by creating a network of independently operated outlets that carry your brand and follow your standards. It's a popular model for businesses looking to expand geographically. For social enterprises, franchising can be particularly effective when it provides local entrepreneurs with an opportunity to create impact within their communities.

Example: Aravind Eye Care in India

Aravind Eye Care, founded by Dr. Govindappa Venkataswamy, is an eye hospital system that provides affordable eye care to millions in India. Aravind expanded through a franchise-like model where hospitals are independently operated but adhere to strict processes and standards to ensure high-quality, low-cost care. Today, Aravind performs millions of eye surgeries each year, demonstrating how social enterprises can scale through franchising without compromising their mission.

Tip: Franchising can be resource-intensive but powerful for scaling impact when carefully planned. Invest in training, clear standards, and a support system to help franchisees stay aligned with your mission.

Case Studies of Scaled Social Enterprises

Let's dive into the stories of social enterprises that have successfully scaled while staying true to their mission. These examples illustrate how different approaches to scaling can amplify impact and help businesses reach new heights without compromising their values.

1. TOMS Shoes: Scaling with a Simple Mission

TOMS Shoes launched with a clear, simple model: for every pair of shoes purchased, TOMS would donate a pair to a child in need. This "One for One" concept resonated with consumers and helped TOMS grow rapidly. As the company scaled, they expanded the model to other areas, such as providing safe water and vision services.

Scaling Strategy: TOMS kept its mission simple, making it easy to communicate as they expanded. By staying focused on the core "One for One" concept, they were able to maintain their brand identity even as they diversified their offerings.

Lesson: Clear, straightforward missions make it easier to scale without confusing customers. If your mission is easy to understand and communicate, it's easier to maintain consistency as you grow.

2. Warby Parker: Building a Mission-Driven Culture

Warby Parker is known for its affordable, stylish eyewear and its mission to provide glasses to people in need. Warby Parker's "Buy a Pair, Give a Pair" model mirrors TOMS' approach, but they also built a strong culture of social responsibility within their team. This commitment to impact is reflected in their hiring practices, customer service, and partnerships.

Scaling Strategy: Warby Parker scaled by building a culture of social responsibility from day one. Every employee understands the company's mission, which helps ensure that values are upheld at every level.

Lesson: A strong internal culture rooted in your mission can help you scale without losing sight of your values. Hire people who believe in your mission, and make impact a part of every role within your organization.

3. BioLite: A Two-Tier Revenue Model

BioLite started as a social enterprise focused on providing clean energy solutions to off-grid communities. They developed a wood-burning stove that converts heat into electricity, allowing families to cook safely while charging small devices. To fund their impact in developing areas, BioLite created a two-tier model: they sell camping stoves and solar products in developed markets to support their social impact projects in off-grid regions.

Scaling Strategy: BioLite used a diversified revenue model to fund its impact. Profits from their retail side subsidize their projects in off-grid communities, creating a sustainable way to scale.

Lesson: Diversified revenue models can provide financial stability and support impact goals. Consider how your products or services might serve different markets in ways that fuel both profit and impact.

Technology as a Tool for Expansion

In today's digital age, technology offers powerful ways to scale impact-driven businesses. From social media to e-commerce platforms, digital tools allow you to reach more people, operate efficiently, and even track your impact. Let's explore how to leverage technology to expand your social enterprise.

1. Digital Platforms for Global Reach

Digital platforms such as social media, e-commerce, and crowdfunding can help you connect with audiences around the world. Social media lets you communicate directly with consumers, build a loyal community, and share your mission. E-commerce platforms allow you to sell products internationally, making it easier to expand without needing a physical presence in every region.

Case Study: Who Gives a Crap's Crowdfunding Success

Who Gives a Crap is an eco-friendly toilet paper company that donates half of its profits to help build toilets in underserved communities. To launch their product, they used crowdfunding, creating a fun, engaging campaign that went viral. The crowdfunding approach allowed them to raise the necessary funds and attract a community of impact-driven consumers who continue to support their mission.

Tip: When using digital platforms, focus on authenticity. Share stories, highlight your impact, and engage your audience in meaningful ways to build trust and loyalty.

2. Leveraging E-Commerce to Scale Sustainably

E-commerce is one of the most accessible ways for social enterprises to reach conscious consumers worldwide. Platforms like Shopify, Etsy, and Amazon can serve as low-cost entry points to global markets, allowing you to grow sustainably by building an online customer base.

Example: Allbirds' E-Commerce Expansion

Allbirds, a sustainable shoe company, started with e-commerce as their primary sales channel. By focusing on an online-first strategy, they reached eco-conscious consumers worldwide while minimizing their carbon footprint. Allbirds used e-commerce not only to sell products but also to tell their story, highlighting their sustainable materials and commitment to the environment. This online-first approach enabled them to scale quickly while maintaining their mission.

Tip: Use your e-commerce platform as a space to educate customers about your mission. Highlight your impact metrics, share customer stories, and make it easy for visitors to understand how their purchase contributes to a bigger cause.

3. Data Analytics for Impact Tracking and Decision-Making

Data analytics tools can provide valuable insights into customer behavior, product performance, and impact. By tracking data, you can make informed decisions about where to expand, which products resonate most, and where you might need to adjust your approach. Impact data, in particular, allows you to communicate progress to customers and investors, showing how your business makes a difference.

Example: Tracking Impact for Continuous Improvement

A company that produces solar lanterns for rural communities used data analytics to understand which regions had the highest demand and impact potential. They tracked metrics like the number of households served, carbon emissions reduced, and customer feedback on product effectiveness. This data allowed them to refine their approach, target high-impact regions, and continuously improve their product.

Tip: Start with simple metrics that are relevant to your mission and business model. Use data not just to measure impact but to identify areas for growth and improvement.

Bringing It All Together

Scaling a social enterprise is about balancing growth with integrity. By choosing strategies like strategic partnerships, licensing, and leveraging technology, you can expand your impact without losing sight of your mission. Each approach to scaling comes with its own set of challenges and rewards, but when you prioritize your values and keep impact at the center, growth becomes a means to amplify your positive influence.

Remember, scaling isn't just about getting bigger; it's about making a bigger difference. By learning from successful social enterprises, using technology to reach new audiences, and maintaining a clear focus on your mission, you'll be well-equipped to grow sustainably and with purpose.

So go out there, scale with intention, and continue building a business that not only thrives but also inspires meaningful change.

CHAPTER 13

Navigating Challenges and Staying Resilient

Building a social enterprise is a balancing act. It's about staying true to your mission while also making enough money to keep the doors open. As you grow, you'll face pressure to prioritize profits or scale quickly, which can lead to difficult decisions about your values and goals. But here's the good news: challenges don't have to derail you. With the right approach, they can strengthen your resilience, deepen your connection with your mission, and build even greater trust within your community.

In this chapter, we're going to explore how to balance profit and purpose, avoid mission drift as you scale, and build a loyal community around your brand. Let's dig into what it means to stay resilient and focused, even when the going gets tough.

Balancing Profit and Purpose

One of the most common challenges for social enterprises is balancing financial sustainability with impact. You need to generate revenue to grow and reach more people, but you also want to stay committed to your values. The key to balancing profit and purpose is recognizing that financial health doesn't have to come at the expense of your mission. Here are some practical strategies for achieving this balance.

1. Create a Revenue Model Aligned with Your Mission

Your revenue model can either support or undermine your mission, depending on how it's structured. To keep profit and purpose in sync, build a revenue model that naturally reinforces your impact goals. This might mean offering products or services that reflect your values, or designing your business to generate revenue in ways that directly benefit your mission.

Case Study: Who Gives a Crap and Their Mission-Driven Model

Who Gives a Crap sells eco-friendly toilet paper and donates 50% of their profits to help build toilets in communities without access to sanitation. Their business model is straightforward, and every sale directly supports their mission. By choosing a product that aligns with their purpose and setting up a profit-sharing model, they've created a revenue stream that feels inherently mission-driven. Customers can easily see how their purchase contributes to the greater good, which builds loyalty and trust.

Tip: Think about how your revenue model can reflect your mission. If you're an eco-friendly brand, for example, consider incorporating eco-conscious production or a donation strategy that aligns with environmental causes. A model that naturally reinforces your purpose helps you maintain mission alignment as you grow.

2. Prioritize Long-Term Financial Health Over Quick Wins

In the world of social entrepreneurship, it's tempting to chase fast profits to keep the business afloat, especially in the early days. But focusing too much on short-term gains can pull you away from your mission. Instead, look for sustainable, long-term growth strategies that align with your values. Slow, intentional growth may take time, but it ensures you're building a foundation that supports both profit and purpose.

Anecdote: A Small Sustainable Brand's Slow-and-Steady Growth

I once worked with a small sustainable clothing brand that was offered a lucrative deal with a major retailer. But to meet the retailer's demand, they would have had to compromise on their commitment to ethical sourcing and sustainable production. After much deliberation, they decided to pass on the deal and focus on growing gradually with local shops and online sales. This decision was tough, but it ultimately helped them build a strong, mission-driven brand that attracted a loyal customer base. Today, they're thriving, and the slow growth has allowed them to stay true to their values.

Tip: Don't feel pressured to grow faster than you're ready for. Sometimes, saying "no" to big opportunities can be the best way to protect your mission and maintain long-term sustainability.

3. Reinforce Your Commitment to Impact with Financial Goals

Balancing profit and purpose doesn't mean neglecting financial health; it means setting financial goals that enable your impact. For example, you might aim for a specific profit margin that allows you to reinvest in your mission, expand your programs, or build a cash reserve for stability. Financial goals that support your mission rather than competing with it will keep your business focused on both impact and sustainability.

Example: Setting Financial Targets That Fund Impact Initiatives

A fair-trade coffee company I know sets aside 10% of profits to invest in programs for their farming communities, such as healthcare, education, and infrastructure. By building this allocation into their financial goals, they've found a way to make profit and purpose work together. This approach also shows customers and stakeholders that their financial success directly fuels their mission, creating trust and goodwill.

Avoiding Mission Drift

As your social enterprise grows, you'll likely face decisions and pressures that could pull you away from your original mission. Mission drift happens when a business begins to prioritize profits or expansion at the expense of its core values. Staying intentional about your mission is essential to scaling with integrity.

1. Define Your "Non-Negotiables" Early

One of the best ways to avoid mission drift is to define your "non-negotiables" from the start. These are the values, principles, or practices you're unwilling to compromise on, no matter how much your business grows. Whether it's ethical sourcing, community partnerships, or environmental sustainability, defining these non-negotiables creates a framework that guides decision-making and keeps your mission front and center.

Tip: Write down your non-negotiables and share them with your team, investors, and partners. When everyone understands your core commitments, it's easier to hold each other accountable and stay aligned with your mission.

Anecdote: A Social Enterprise's Commitment to Local Production

I worked with a social enterprise that makes handcrafted home goods and was committed to supporting local artisans. As demand grew, they were approached by a factory overseas that could produce items at a much lower cost. But after weighing the pros and cons, they decided to stick with local production because it was one of their non-negotiables. This decision preserved their mission, helped support the community, and deepened their customers' loyalty.

2. Set Mission-Based Performance Indicators

Growth metrics like revenue and customer acquisition are important, but for a social enterprise, they're only part of the picture. To keep your mission at the heart of your growth, create mission-based performance indicators that measure your impact. These could include metrics like carbon emissions saved, number of lives impacted, or hours of job training provided. These indicators remind you and your team that impact is just as important as profit.

Example: Impact Metrics in Action

A clean energy company I know uses carbon emissions reductions as a core performance indicator. While they track sales and revenue, they also set annual targets for the amount of emissions saved through their products. This metric keeps them focused on their mission, and it's a powerful tool for communicating impact to customers, investors, and partners.

Tip: Choose impact metrics that align directly with your mission and goals. Track them with the same rigor as financial metrics to keep impact at the heart of your growth strategy.

3. Be Selective About Partners and Investors

Partnerships and investments can help you scale, but they can also lead to mission drift if your values aren't aligned. Be intentional about choosing partners and investors who understand and respect your mission. Look for people and organizations that share your vision and are committed to impact-driven growth.

Case Study: Ben & Jerry's Selective Partnerships

Ben & Jerry's has long been a pioneer in social responsibility, and they're very selective about the companies they partner with. When they were acquired by Unilever, they negotiated terms that allowed them to maintain an independent board dedicated to social mission oversight. This agreement allowed Ben & Jerry's to scale globally without compromising their values, demonstrating how selective partnerships can support mission integrity even during rapid expansion.

Tip: Don't rush into partnerships for the sake of growth. Take time to vet partners and investors, ensuring their values and vision align with yours.

Building Community and Trust

Building a loyal community is one of the most valuable assets for a social enterprise. When people trust your brand, they become your advocates, supporters, and repeat customers. Strong community engagement not only strengthens your mission but also provides resilience during challenging times.

1. Foster Transparent Communication

Transparency builds trust, and it's especially important in social enterprises where people want to know their support is making a difference. Be open about your progress, challenges, and the impact you're creating. Share both the successes and the setbacks, showing your audience that you're committed to accountability.

Example: Everlane's "Radical Transparency" Approach

Everlane, a sustainable clothing brand, practices "radical transparency" by sharing information about their factories, production costs, and impact goals. They even reveal the cost breakdown for each product, showing customers exactly where their money goes. This level of transparency has built a loyal community of customers who appreciate the brand's honesty and commitment to sustainability.

Tip: Consider publishing regular impact reports, blog posts, or social media updates to keep your community informed. Share specific data, stories, and insights to show that you're committed to accountability and improvement.

2. Engage Your Community in Your Mission

When people feel like they're part of your mission, they're more likely to support your brand. Find ways to engage your community in meaningful ways, whether it's through events, volunteer opportunities, or social media challenges. Give them a role in your journey, and celebrate their contributions.

Anecdote: A Social Enterprise's Community Garden Project

A friend of mine started a social enterprise focused on sustainable agriculture. To engage her community, she launched a "Plant a Garden" challenge on social media, encouraging followers to start their own small vegetable gardens and share photos of their progress. The response was overwhelming, with hundreds of people participating and sharing their experiences. This engagement built a sense of community and strengthened people's connection to the brand's mission of sustainability.

Tip: Encourage your audience to be part of your mission in small but meaningful ways. Community-driven challenges, events, and campaigns help foster a sense of ownership and loyalty.

3. Celebrate Milestones and Impact Together

Celebrating milestones isn't just about acknowledging your success; it's a chance to thank your supporters and remind them of the impact they're helping create. Whether it's reaching a fundraising goal, completing a project, or achieving a new impact milestone, take the time to celebrate with your community.

Example: Celebrating Milestones with the "Thank You" Campaign

Charity: Water, a nonprofit focused on providing clean water, regularly celebrates milestones with their supporters. When they reach a funding goal or complete a project, they share photos, stories, and videos to show the difference their community has made.

These celebrations reinforce the impact of their work and give supporters a tangible sense of accomplishment.

Tip: Mark milestones in meaningful ways, like sharing success stories, hosting virtual events, or sending personalized thank-you messages. Celebrating together strengthens your community's commitment to your mission.

Bringing It All Together

Running a social enterprise is filled with unique challenges, but each one is an opportunity to reinforce your mission, build resilience, and deepen trust with your community. By balancing profit and purpose, staying vigilant against mission drift, and nurturing a loyal community, you'll create a brand that's both sustainable and impactful.

Remember, resilience isn't just about enduring challenges—it's about growing stronger because of them. When you stay committed to your values and engage your community in meaningful ways, your social enterprise can thrive and make a lasting difference in the world. So take on each challenge with confidence, keep your mission at the heart of everything you do, and let your community be your greatest ally in creating change.

CHAPTER 14

The Global Landscape of Social Entrepreneurship

Social entrepreneurship has taken off around the world in recent years. Today, social entrepreneurs are working in every corner of the globe to address issues like climate change, poverty, access to healthcare, and educational inequality. But here's the thing: the challenges, opportunities, and resources available to social enterprises vary widely depending on where you're located. Each region brings its own unique context, from supportive government policies to cultural nuances, and understanding these regional dynamics is essential for any social entrepreneur looking to make a lasting impact.

In this chapter, we'll explore how social entrepreneurship looks across different regions, the policies and incentives available worldwide, and ways to connect with the global network of social innovators. Whether you're launching a venture in your hometown or looking to expand internationally, this chapter will help you navigate the global landscape and find the right opportunities to make an impact.

Regional Opportunities and Challenges

Social entrepreneurship is a global movement, but it doesn't operate in a vacuum. Economic, cultural, and political factors shape the way social enterprises work in each region, presenting both opportunities and challenges. Let's explore some of the unique aspects of social entrepreneurship in different parts of the world and how businesses can adapt.

1. Africa: Growing Demand for Social Innovation

Africa has one of the world's youngest populations and a high demand for solutions to pressing issues like access to clean water, affordable healthcare, and renewable energy. Social enterprises in Africa have a tremendous opportunity to create impact, but they often face challenges in funding, infrastructure, and scaling.

Case Study: M-KOPA Solar in East Africa

M-KOPA Solar is a social enterprise that provides affordable, solar-powered home systems to off-grid households in Kenya, Uganda, and Tanzania. M-KOPA uses a "pay-as-you-go" model that allows customers to pay for solar energy in small installments through mobile money. This approach has made clean energy accessible to low-income households, reducing reliance on harmful kerosene lamps and improving quality of life. By understanding the local context—both the demand for affordable energy and the popularity of mobile money—M-KOPA developed a model that meets a critical need in East Africa.

Tip: When working in Africa, think about scalable solutions that address essential needs and leverage local systems, like mobile money. Adaptability and local relevance are key to success.

2. Asia: High-Tech Solutions and Cultural Sensitivity

Asia is home to diverse economies, from rapidly growing tech hubs like India and Singapore to countries with rural populations facing poverty and healthcare gaps. Social entrepreneurs in Asia often incorporate technology to address challenges, and the region's strong emphasis on community means that businesses rooted in cultural understanding are more likely to succeed.

Example: Goonj in India

Goonj is a nonprofit organization in India that uses urban surplus materials (like clothing and fabrics) to support rural development initiatives. Instead of simply providing aid, Goonj partners with rural communities to address local challenges through a "Cloth for Work" program, where people receive clothing in exchange for participating in community improvement projects. This culturally sensitive approach has transformed the way rural communities in India see themselves, empowering them to become part of the solution.

Tip: In Asia, it's essential to recognize cultural nuances and integrate local customs into your approach. Solutions that honor traditions and community values often resonate more deeply.

3. Europe: Supportive Policies and a Focus on Sustainability

Europe is a leader in sustainable and social entrepreneurship, with many governments offering support through grants, certifications, and incentives. The European Union (EU) has introduced policies to support social enterprises and encourage sustainable business practices. Social ventures in Europe are also increasingly focused on environmental issues, as climate awareness is high across the continent.

Case Study: Rubies in the Rubble in the UK

Rubies in the Rubble is a British social enterprise that tackles food waste by making chutneys, jams, and relishes from surplus produce that would otherwise go to waste. Their mission is supported by the EU's push for sustainability and circular economy practices, and the UK's food-conscious consumers have been enthusiastic supporters. By aligning with both local and regional sustainability goals, Rubies in the Rubble has found a receptive market and expanded its product line.

Tip: If you're working in Europe, take advantage of sustainability policies, funding opportunities, and growing consumer awareness. Aligning with EU goals for social and environmental impact can open doors and build brand loyalty.

4. Latin America: Tackling Inequality Through Grassroots Efforts

Latin America faces challenges with economic inequality, access to education, and healthcare. Many social enterprises in the region are grassroots initiatives focused on economic empowerment, agriculture, and community-driven development. Latin American social enterprises often emphasize collaboration with local communities, working alongside them to address systemic issues.

Example: Laboratoria in Peru and Mexico

Laboratoria is a social enterprise that provides coding education to women in Latin America, empowering them with skills to enter the tech workforce. By focusing on low-income women, Laboratoria addresses both gender inequality and economic opportunity. The organization has partnerships with local tech companies, allowing students to transition directly into the workforce. Laboratoria's model demonstrates how social enterprises in Latin America can address inequality by offering practical, job-focused education.

Tip: In Latin America, building trust with communities and establishing local partnerships is critical. By focusing on community needs and involving local stakeholders, social enterprises can create long-term, sustainable impact.

Policy and Government Support for Social Ventures

Many countries are beginning to recognize the value of social entrepreneurship and have introduced policies, incentives, and certifications to support social enterprises. Understanding these options can help you take advantage of government support and create a stronger foundation for your mission.

1. Certifications and Legal Structures for Social Enterprises

Several countries offer specialized certifications or legal structures that recognize businesses with a social or environmental mission. These certifications can offer benefits like tax breaks, access to grants, and a stronger reputation with socially-conscious consumers.

- **B Corporation Certification (Global)**: Certified B Corporations (B Corps) meet high standards of social and environmental performance, accountability, and transparency. The B Corp certification is available internationally and provides credibility, access to a global network, and often attracts impact-driven investors.
- **Benefit Corporation Status (US)**: In the United States, social enterprises can register as Benefit Corporations, a legal status that allows companies to prioritize social impact alongside profit. Benefit Corporations commit to considering their impact on society and the environment in their business decisions.
- **Community Interest Company (CIC) in the UK**: CIC is a legal structure for social enterprises in the United Kingdom. CICs operate as limited companies but have additional obligations to use their profits for public good. CIC status gives social enterprises credibility with customers and access to specific grants and funding options.

Tip: Consider whether a legal status or certification is beneficial for your enterprise. These designations can strengthen your brand, appeal to conscious consumers, and open doors to resources specifically for social enterprises.

2. Tax Incentives and Grants for Social Enterprises

Governments around the world are starting to offer tax incentives and grants to social enterprises, encouraging businesses to address social and environmental issues. For example:

- **France's Social Solidarity Economy**: France provides

grants and tax breaks for organizations in the "social and solidarity economy" (SSE). These incentives are available for social enterprises tackling issues like environmental sustainability, poverty, and healthcare.
- **Canada's Social Enterprise Development Fund**: Canada has introduced various funding programs for social enterprises, including grants, low-interest loans, and impact investing initiatives. The Social Enterprise Development Fund, for instance, provides funding to social enterprises that demonstrate a commitment to local and social impact.

Example: Leveraging Incentives in France

A social enterprise in France working on renewable energy solutions applied for funding through the country's SSE grants. With the support of these grants, they were able to scale their solar panel distribution to rural communities, making clean energy more accessible. The grant funding also provided financial stability, allowing them to reinvest in further expansion without losing sight of their mission.

Tip: Research tax incentives and grants in your country or region. These resources can provide financial relief and support for growth, helping you expand your impact while remaining financially sustainable.

3. Policy Support for Sustainable Development Goals (SDGs)

The UN Sustainable Development Goals (SDGs) have been adopted by countries worldwide, and many governments now offer support for businesses that align with these goals. Social enterprises addressing SDGs like poverty, clean water, or affordable energy may have access to additional resources, funding, and recognition in countries prioritizing sustainable development.

Example: Using SDG Alignment to Secure Support in India

A social enterprise in India focused on clean water aligned its mission with SDG 6: Clean Water and Sanitation. By highlighting this alignment, the enterprise gained access to government funding for water infrastructure development in rural areas. The alignment with SDGs not only made the social enterprise eligible for support but also attracted impact investors looking to support ventures contributing to the global goals.

Tip: If your enterprise aligns with specific SDGs, make this clear in your funding applications and marketing materials. Highlighting SDG alignment can open doors to government support and partnerships with international organizations.

Connecting with the Global Network

One of the greatest strengths of social entrepreneurship is its global community. There are international organizations, accelerators, and networks dedicated to helping social enterprises thrive. Here's how you can connect with the global social entrepreneurship network to access resources, mentorship, and support.

1. International Organizations for Social Impact

Several international organizations focus on supporting social enterprises by providing funding, mentorship, and visibility. Some of the top organizations include:

- **Ashoka**: Ashoka is one of the world's largest networks of social entrepreneurs. They support innovators who are addressing social problems with creative, scalable solutions, offering fellowships, mentorship, and connections with other changemakers.
- **Skoll Foundation**: The Skoll Foundation funds social entrepreneurs who are tackling critical global issues. Skoll Award recipients gain access to funding, resources, and networking opportunities, which can be transformative for scaling impact.

Example: An Ashoka Fellow's Journey

One entrepreneur I know became an Ashoka Fellow after launching a mobile education platform for underserved communities. Through Ashoka, she received mentorship from industry leaders, funding to scale her platform, and opportunities to connect with like-minded entrepreneurs worldwide. This support helped her grow her enterprise and reach new communities, amplifying her impact on education access.

Tip: Research international organizations that align with your mission and apply for programs or fellowships. These networks provide not just funding but also credibility, mentorship, and lasting connections.

2. Impact Accelerators and Incubators

Impact accelerators and incubators provide social enterprises with access to mentorship, funding, and a structured growth path. These programs are designed specifically for impact-driven businesses and offer a wealth of resources for scaling.

- **Echoing Green**: Echoing Green provides seed funding and support for emerging social enterprises. Their accelerator program offers mentorship, leadership development, and funding for social entrepreneurs tackling pressing global issues.
- **Acumen Academy**: Acumen Academy runs accelerator programs for social enterprises working on issues like poverty, healthcare, and education. Their programs are structured to help businesses scale sustainably and create measurable impact.

Anecdote: A Social Enterprise's Journey with Acumen

A social enterprise focused on affordable healthcare in Southeast Asia joined Acumen's accelerator program, which provided not only funding but also a curriculum on scaling impact sustainably. The program connected them with mentors and industry experts, helping them refine their business model and expand their reach.

Today, they're providing healthcare to thousands of people across rural communities.

Tip: Explore accelerator programs that align with your mission. These programs offer structured support, guidance, and resources to help you scale effectively.

3. Online Communities and Networking Platforms

There are several online communities and platforms where social entrepreneurs can connect, share insights, and find collaboration opportunities. Some popular options include:

- **Impact Hub**: A global network of spaces for social innovators, offering co-working spaces, events, and resources. Impact Hub connects changemakers from all over the world.
- **Changemakers by Ashoka**: An online platform for social entrepreneurs to collaborate, share ideas, and learn from one another.

Example: Building a Support Network through Impact Hub

A friend of mine launched a social enterprise in sustainable packaging and joined her local Impact Hub. Through the network, she connected with fellow entrepreneurs, attended workshops, and even found a business partner. The connections she made at Impact Hub provided invaluable support as she navigated the challenges of building a purpose-driven business.

Tip: Join an online community or attend virtual events to connect with other social entrepreneurs. Networking is one of the best ways to learn, find partners, and gain inspiration from others in the field.

Bringing It All Together

Navigating the global landscape of social entrepreneurship requires an understanding of the regional dynamics, policies, and networks that shape the field. By recognizing regional opportunities and challenges, leveraging government support, and connecting with the global community, you can strengthen your social enterprise and maximize your impact.

Remember, social entrepreneurship is about collaboration as much as it is about innovation. You're part of a global movement of people who believe in creating positive change, and the more you connect, learn, and grow within this network, the greater your impact will be. Embrace the resources, insights, and inspiration available to you around the world, and let them guide your journey toward building a business that changes the world.

Conclusion

Your Role as a Catalyst for Change

The journey of building a business with impact isn't easy. It's a path of constant learning, adaptation, and persistence. But if there's one thing that social entrepreneurs and purpose-driven investors have in common, it's a deep-rooted belief in the power of business to create positive change. Each step you take brings us closer to a future where profit and purpose go hand in hand, where communities thrive, and where our planet is protected for generations to come.

As you wrap up this book, I want to leave you with an understanding of the unique and critical role you play in building a more sustainable, inclusive world. You're not just starting or funding a business; you're becoming a catalyst for change. This isn't a role to take lightly, but it's also one to embrace with optimism and hope.

Let's dive into the final pieces of inspiration, community, and resources that will keep you going on your journey to build a business that truly changes the world.

A CALL TO ACTION FOR ENTREPRENEURS AND INVESTORS

Entrepreneurs and investors have a special power: they're the ones who turn ideas into reality, who take risks, and who are willing to challenge the status quo. In a world facing so many pressing issues—climate change, inequality, lack of access to basic needs—you are the ones willing to step up and say, "I want to be part of the solution."

1. Entrepreneurs: Building with Purpose

If you're an entrepreneur, know that you are on the front lines of change. Your ideas, energy, and resilience are what fuel impact-driven businesses. Each decision you make—whether it's about sourcing materials, hiring practices, or community engagement—is an opportunity to make a difference. But it's also a responsibility.

Anecdote: The Journey of a Young Social Entrepreneur

I once met a young entrepreneur who launched a biodegradable packaging company. She started small, working from her kitchen and experimenting with sustainable materials. Her motivation came from a love for the ocean and a frustration with the plastic waste crisis. Today, her company supplies eco-friendly packaging to dozens of local restaurants. Her journey hasn't been easy; she's faced setbacks with production, funding, and sourcing. But every time she thought about giving up, she reminded herself of the impact she was making. That purpose kept her going and ultimately drove her success.

Tip: When you face challenges, return to your mission. Remind yourself why you started and who you're working to help. This "why" will be your fuel, especially when the road gets tough.

2. Investors: Funding the Future

If you're an investor, your role is just as critical. By choosing to fund impact-driven businesses, you're helping to shape the future. Each investment you make has the potential to amplify impact and set an example for others. You're not just providing capital; you're providing a vote of confidence in a better world.

Example: Impact Investment for Education Access

A group of impact investors once pooled their resources to fund an ed-tech startup focused on creating accessible, affordable online courses for low-income communities. They saw the startup not only as a financial opportunity but as a way to make quality education available to more people. That startup has since grown, reaching thousands of students who would otherwise have no access to formal education. The investors didn't just fund a business; they made a difference in countless lives.

Tip: Look beyond financial returns. Consider the social or environmental impact as part of your ROI, and remember that investing in impact-driven ventures doesn't just change the world—it often leads to long-term, sustainable growth.

Continuous Learning and Community Support

No one builds a better world alone. Whether you're an entrepreneur or an investor, you need a community that will support you, provide insights, and lift you up when things get difficult. And the truth is, the world of social entrepreneurship is constantly evolving. New challenges and opportunities emerge every day, and continuous learning is essential.

1. Embrace Lifelong Learning

The journey of creating a social enterprise or supporting one as an investor is full of learning curves. Embrace the fact that you'll never have all the answers, and be open to continuous growth. Read up on industry trends, attend conferences, and engage with mentors who've walked the path before you. The more you learn, the better equipped you'll be to adapt and innovate.

Anecdote: A Founder's Story of Reinvention

One founder I know started a social enterprise focused on organic farming. When they first launched, they relied on traditional farming techniques but quickly realized they weren't yielding enough to sustain the business. Instead of giving up, they dove into research and learned about permaculture, a regenerative agricultural practice. By adapting their methods, they not only improved crop yields but also increased their impact on soil health and biodiversity. Embracing lifelong learning allowed them to overcome a challenge and turn it into an opportunity for greater impact.

Tip: Treat every challenge as a lesson. When things don't go as planned, ask yourself, "What can I learn from this?" This mindset will help you stay resilient and innovative.

2. Build a Supportive Network

Having a supportive network is invaluable. Surround yourself with people who share your values, who understand your mission, and who can offer guidance when you need it most. This community could include fellow social entrepreneurs, investors, mentors, or even customers who believe in your work.

Example: The Power of Peer Support

There's a group of social entrepreneurs I know who meet monthly to discuss their challenges, successes, and ideas. One member was struggling with a product launch, while another had successfully launched multiple products. By sharing their experiences, the second entrepreneur offered actionable advice that helped the first one navigate the challenges. The network not only provided practical support but also boosted each entrepreneur's morale and reinforced their commitment to their missions.

Tip: Don't hesitate to reach out and build relationships within the social entrepreneurship community. Join online forums, attend meetups, and consider joining a local or global impact network.

3. Seek Mentorship and Pay It Forward

Mentorship can provide valuable insights and guidance, especially when you're facing uncharted territory. Look for mentors who understand the nuances of social entrepreneurship, and be open to their advice. And once you've gained experience, consider becoming a mentor yourself. Sharing what you've learned can have a ripple effect, empowering other change-makers to keep pushing forward.

Anecdote: Mentorship Across Generations

I once met a young founder who started a social enterprise focused on providing career training for at-risk youth. She was mentored by a seasoned social entrepreneur who had built a similar program years before. Through regular mentorship sessions, the young founder gained insights on scaling, navigating partnerships, and managing community relationships. Years later, she became a mentor herself, passing on the lessons she'd learned to a new generation of social entrepreneurs.

Tip: Seek out mentors, and when you're ready, give back by mentoring others. Mentorship is a powerful way to build a strong, supportive community of change-makers.

Joining the Movement for a Better World

At the end of the day, social entrepreneurship isn't just about one business or one investor; it's about creating a global movement. You're part of something much bigger—a collective of people who believe in the power of business to solve real-world problems and make a positive impact. By working together, sharing knowledge, and supporting one another, we can create a world where social impact and profit go hand in hand.

1. Tap into Global Resources and Networks

There are countless resources available to support social entrepreneurs and investors. From online platforms and accelerators to international organizations and conferences, you have a wealth of tools at your fingertips. These networks can help you learn, find funding, build partnerships, and connect with people who share your vision.

Example: The Support of the Global Impact Network

Impact Hub is a global network that offers coworking spaces, events, and resources for social entrepreneurs. I know a founder who started working at Impact Hub in her city and soon discovered she had access to a worldwide network of change-makers. Through this network, she found mentors, investors, and partners who helped her scale her enterprise internationally. The support and connections she found within this global community were instrumental in her growth.

Tip: Explore networks and organizations that align with your mission. Platforms like Impact Hub, Ashoka, and Skoll Foundation provide invaluable resources and support for social entrepreneurs.

2. Recognize the Power of Collective Action

One of the most beautiful aspects of social entrepreneurship is the way it brings people together for a common cause. When entrepreneurs, investors, communities, and governments work together, the impact multiplies. Remember, your work isn't isolated—it's part of a larger movement toward a better world.

Anecdote: A Community-Driven Success Story

I once visited a small town where a group of local businesses banded together to reduce plastic waste. Each business committed to using biodegradable packaging and holding workshops on sustainability. Customers started noticing, spreading the word, and bringing their own containers to the shops. This collective action inspired other businesses in nearby towns to adopt similar practices. Together, they created a ripple effect that not only reduced waste but also fostered a culture of sustainability throughout the region.

Tip: Look for opportunities to collaborate with others who share your mission. Collective action often has a greater impact than individual efforts.

3. Embrace Your Role as a Changemaker

Finally, remember that you are a changemaker. Every decision you make, every person you hire, every partnership you form—all of these choices are part of your role in creating a better world. Embrace this responsibility with humility, passion, and a willingness to learn. The world needs people like you, who believe in the power of purpose-driven work and are willing to take risks to make a difference.

Tip: Reflect regularly on your impact and remind yourself why you started. Keeping your mission close will inspire you to keep moving forward, even on the toughest days.

Final Words

As you close this book, take a moment to recognize the incredible journey you're embarking on as a social entrepreneur or impact-driven investor. You're stepping into a role that has the power to transform lives, strengthen communities, and inspire others to believe in the power of business as a force for good.

Remember, this journey isn't about perfection—it's about progress. It's about taking small steps toward a bigger vision and building a business that contributes to a world where everyone thrives. Surround yourself with people who believe in your mission, stay open to learning, and embrace the ups and downs with resilience and courage.

The world is waiting for your impact. So go out there, build a business that changes the world, and know that you're part of a movement that's making the future brighter for us all.

www.ingramcontent.com/pod-product-compliance
Lightning Source LLC
Chambersburg PA
CBHW070143230526
45471CB00002B/501